THE 50,000 YEAR
JOURNEY
of the
KNUSLI FAMILY

Author
RONALD EARL NICELY

The map on the front cover shows the trail of the Knusli family journey from Eastern Central Africa northward and eastward across the continents and then across the ████ Ocean to America and to Lancaster, PA. It was not one long journey but a journey of time with many stops and starts in many different parts of the world. The information that established the very early journey locations came from the results of testing the male Y-DNA of the author of the book. The testing was completed by Family Tree DNA and the results were submitted to the National Geographic Genographic study and to a J2 Haplogroup Y-DNA study that was being undertaken in Greece. These two studies gave me information on the locations where my DNA was located. Comparison of my DNA to samples that were time dated and matched indicated places around the world where my DNA was present. This location information was used to trace our path prior to the arrival in Switzerland. The path from Switzerland and the rest of the journey was indicated in many different reports and in family history.

The picture on the map in the bottom right represents the early beginnings of the trek out of Africa where they were hunters following the animals as they moved north, the middle picture represents the Anatolia area, where they were cave dwellers. The last picture on the top left is of the Anthony A. Nicely family of Ligonier PA and is used as a representation of our many families in America.

WE ARE THE CHOSEN...

We are the chosen. In each family there is one who seems called to find the ancestors. To put flesh on their bones and make them live again, to tell the family story and to feel that somehow they know and approve.

Doing genealogy is not a cold gathering of facts but, instead, breathing life into all who have gone before. We are the storytellers of the tribe. All tribes have one. We have been called, as it were, by our genes. Those who have gone before cry out to us, "Tell our story!" So, we do.

In finding them, we somehow find ourselves. How many graves have I stood before now and cried? I have lost count. How many times have I told the ancestors, "You have a wonderful family; you would be proud of us." How many times have I walked up to a grave and felt somehow there was love there for me? I cannot say.

It goes beyond just documenting facts. It goes to who I am and why do I do the things I do. It goes to seeing a cemetery about to be lost forever to weeds and indifference and saying, "I can't let this happen." The bones here are bones of my bone and flesh of my flesh. It goes to doing something about it. It goes to pride in what our ancestors were able to accomplish, how they contributed to what we are today. It goes to respecting their hardships and losses, their never giving in or giving up, their resoluteness to go on and build a life for their family.

It goes to deep pride that the fathers fought and some died to make and keep us a Nation. It goes to a deep and immense understanding that they were doing it for us. It is of equal pride and love that our mothers struggled to give us birth. Without them we could not exist, and so we love each one, as far back as we can reach.

That we might be born who we are. That we might remember them. So we do. With love and caring and scribing each fact of their existence, because we are they and they are the sum of who we are.

So, as a scribe called, I tell the story of my family. It is up to that one called in the next generation to answer the call and take my place in the long line of family storytellers.

That is why I do my family genealogy, and that is what calls those young and old to step up and restore the memory or greet those whom we had never known before.

Author Unknown

To my cousin Kay Houghton
I hope you enjoy reading about our long family journey.
Thanks
Cousin Ron Neely
9/22/14

(See 3 pages inserted inside the back cover)

For comments, questions, and autographed book purchases
Contact Ronald Earl Nicely directly at
nicelyguy@msn.com

This book can also be ordered online at
The Lulu Bookstore at

http://www.lulu.com/shop/shop.ep

or
Nicely (Knusli) Family History Store

http://lulu.com/spotlight/knusli1717

or
as an eBook at one of the following
Amazon Kindle
Sony e-Reader
Barnes and Noble Nook
Kobo (Borders) e-Reader
Google eBook site.

© Copyright 2014 Ronald Earl Nicely

All rights reserved.
No part of this publication may be reproduced, stored in a
retrieval system, or transmitted by any means,
electronic, mechanical, photocopying, recording,
or otherwise, without written permission
from the author.

Print ISBN: 978-1-304-54454-4
eBook ISBN: 978-1-625-17479-6

Dedication & Recognition

This book is dedicated to all the ancestors and the wide spread members of the Knusli family that did research and gratefully supplied information to me that was utilized in developing the history in this book. I also want to recognize the website "Family Tree DNA" who completed the tests on the Knusli family members who submitted their DNA samples for analysis. I also want to recognize the individuals in Greece who worked on the study of the J2 haplogroup, Costa Tsirigakis and Angela Cone for the information they supplied that was helpful in developing some sections of this book. I also need to recognize The National Geographic Genographic Project that supplied volumes of information on the early DNA history of my family line and Dr. Spencer Wells who wrote the book "The Journey of Man" and his DNA research that led to the development of the path that lead to the population of the world and gave me the basis for our long family journey.

I have so many people to thank for their input and assistance that I could not possibly mention them all, but there are some that need to be mentioned. My wife Marian "Chris" Plummer Nicely, who has put up with my research trips and time spent working on the research and writing of the book. My mother (now deceased), Florence Rose McDowell Nicely, who gathered and documented a lot of the information on the Anthony Nicely Sr. branch of the Ligonier, PA family tree over many years and gave me the basis for the start of my research work She was the person that stemmed my interest in knowing more about the family. They say genealogy is a disease you inherit from your ancestors and I would venture to guess I was infected by my mother. LOL. John Robert (Jack) Nicely and Todd Garrett Pelkey, both descendants of the Adam Nicely Jr. Ligonier PA branch, passed on to me almost all of the history for the Adam Nicely Jr. branch of the tree. John Robert and I were the ones who discovered the information that Adam Nicely Sr. was the person who moved to Ligonier and was the father of Anthony Sr. and Adam Jr. On the Whitecrow side of the Kneisle family, Mary

Virginia Scritchfield Wood (now deceased), a descendent of Tsu-Ka-We or Crow as Jacob Nicely was known by his Native American name, had been searching for her ancestors for around twenty years and had accumulated information on Crow's descendants. Her information was passed on to Leora Lacie Whitecrow (now deceased), the wife of Sidney Whitecrow, who became involved a few years back and through the use of the Internet and access to the Native American history files she began to expand the knowledge of Jacob's family. I want to thank Bruno Nuessli, who is a member of the unrelated Nusli family line, of Winterthur, Switzerland, who helped with Y-DNA testing that proved the separation of the Knusli line from the Nusli line. Special thanks goes out to Jake and Sondra Knisely, who helped start all of this interest in the full family line by meeting the Whitecrow family and then finding me. Jake also elected to pay for a Y-DNA test that connected us as cousins and who's historical genealogy data gave me the information to connect to Hans Knussli who was born in 1628 in the Canton of Zurich in Switzerland. Without Jake's efforts in finding me this story could not have been told. I would also like to thank all of the people who have purchased the DNA kits and submitted their DNA to Family Tree DNA for testing. This includes many non Knusli descendants, including Sidney Sacks, who was closely matched and helped indicate a distant cousin connection to the Hebrew line. I would also like to thank all of the family members who got in touch with me and gave me so many stories of the family. The list of names is in no particular order but they were all significant in the process. Jean Aikins Anthony, Rev. Harry Knisely, Glenn Nicely (now deceased), Don Gilmore, James Bernard Niceley, Shirley McQuillis Iscrupe, Harry Loren Knisely, Dwayne Larry Nicely, Robert Knisely, and many others who supplied pieces of their family history that helped to fill the voids in my research.

Contents

Preface x

Introduction xii

Chapter One: DNA and Genealogy 1

Chapter Two: In The Beginning 4

Chapter Three: Mediterranean Sea Area 8
    Anatolia Region 8
    Fertile Crescent Region 9
    Jericho 13

Chapter Four: Journey to Zurich 15

Chapter Five: Zurich Switzerland 18
    The Black Plague 19
    The 1500's in Switzerland 20
    Anabaptist Mennonites in Switzerland 21
    Hans Knussli's Family in Switzerland 22
    Religious Persecution in Switzerland 24

Chapter Six: Alsace, France 28
    The Journey to America 30
    Lancaster, PA 32

Chapter Seven: Antonius Kristopher Knussli Sr. Family 37
    Anna Kneisle Kauffman 37
    Christina Kneisle Haldiman 39
    Johannes Hans Kneisley Sr. 40
    Antonius Kristopher (Anthony) Kneussel Jr. 43
    Elizabeth Kneisly Kauffman 46
    Maria Knussli 47
    Jacob Knussli 47
    Barbara Kneisley Miller 47

Sybilla Kneisley Golladay 49
Mary Kneisley Shelley Landis 50
George H. Kneisley 55
Adam Kneisle 57

Chapter Eight: 1739 Knusli Line 62
Elias Abraham Knisely 62
John Knisely Sr. 64

Chapter Nine: Family Information & Stories From
The Johannes Hans Kneisley Sr. Line 69
Christian Kneisly 69
Sen. George Omit Deise 70
Thomas Alexander Deise 70
Melvin Henry Knisely 71
Jacob Clarence (Jake) Knisely 73
Robert August Knisely 75
Rev. Harry Lee Knisely 76
Michael Douglas Nicely Sr. 77
Alexander (Alex) Knisely 78
Dr. Jonathan Petrus Sandberg Knisely MD 79

Chapter Ten: Family Information & Stories From
The Antonius Kristopher (Anthony) Kneussel Jr. Line 80
Jonas (John) Kniceley Sr. 80
Gillon Truett "Gil" Niceley 81
James "Jim" Bernard Niceley 82
Sen. Frank Samuel Niceley 83
Dwayne Larry Nicely 84

Chapter Eleven: Family Information & Stories From
The George H. Kneisley Line 85
John Kneisly 85
George G. Kneisly 86
Benjamin Franklin Kneisly 86
Harry Loren Kneisly 87

Chapter Twelve: Family Information & Stories From
   The Adam Nicely Line 89
   Anthony Nicely Sr. & Adam Nicely Jr. 89
   Jacob "Crow or Tsu-Ka-We" Nicely 90
   Matthew Gelvin Burkholder Sr. 91
   Josiah G. "Joseph" Nicely & David Curtin Nicely 91
   Frederick Rankin Nicely Sr. 93
   Dr. Robert Frances Nicely Sr. 94
   Dr. William W. McKenna 94
   William Edward Nicely 95
   Ronald Earl Nicely 96
   John Robert "Jack" Nicely 97
   Dr. Robert Frances Nicely Jr. 98
   Don Arthur Gilmore 98
   Todd Garrett Pelkey 99
   Adam Brett Nicely 99

Summary 101

Appendices
   A Jesus's Ancestor Listing 103
   B Middle Eastern Dinner 105
   C Family Veterans of War 106
   D Knusli Books Information 117
   E Family Members in Who's Who 120
   F Family Tree DNA Information 126
   G Possible Knusli ancestors from Zurich 128

References 135

Preface

The information in this book covers the general journey of mankind up to approximately 1300 AD and then after 1300 AD, as we started using a surname the journey gets more specific to the Knusli family journey. Prior to 15,000 to 22,000 years ago, the information covers the general journey of mankind as it developed and evolved from the approximate time of 50,000 years ago. Much of this information was published in the book "Journey of Man", written by Dr. Spencer Wells, which was developed with Y-DNA testing, and explains the development of mankind, the progress, and the path of man's journey as they moved from Africa and into the rest of the continents. Beginning around 15,000 to 22,000 years ago, the data will become slightly more specific to our Knusli Y-DNA ancestors, specifically the male members, and covers the classification Haplogroup J of our Y-DNA. Testing in that area indicated the J Haplogroup began there. The testing of material found in the Fertile Crescent area (Bible Lands) indicates that the Haplogroup classification of J2 began there about 10,000 years ago, which is the next subdivision indicator in the Knusli Y-DNA. Testing since that time has been further refined and our Y-DNA is now classified as J2b2, which is the classification for my Y-DNA and the Y-DNA of the all the male Knusli descendants. Some of the Y-DNA data from this period was taken from an international study in Greece of the specific J2 Haplogroup as it was reported in preliminary releases of the data from the study. This study includes many members of the J2 Haplogroup, which is much broader in scope than just the Knusli Family, but includes the Knusli Family.

The Knusli early family history began to take shape in October 2004 when I was given information about the web site Family Tree DNA and after discussing it with Jacob Knisely, we chose to submit our DNA samples for Y-DNA 12 analysis to determine if we were related. In spite of our efforts, we were unable to find a firm paper trail that would connect us even though we both thought there might be a link. We felt the Y-DNA test would be a good method to confirm or reject a firm family link. Our Y-DNA samples matched

100% on a 12 marker Y-DNA test and confirmed a positive relationship to a common ancestor within 300 years or less, but it also gave us some information I did not understand. The information indicated our Y-DNA was classified as being in the J2 Haplogroup. After searching the internet for information on the J2 Haplogroup in an effort to understand what it meant, I found information taking me back in time to an area of the world where the J2 Haplogroup was located 10,000 years ago. What started out as an effort to connect two individuals as being related, revealed much more information than I had anticipated I would find. My original efforts at genealogy were to find out more about my family and who these people were and perhaps find some additional connections in Europe and to locate stories about my family to understand what they did in their lifetimes. This book will give you most of the information I have been able to locate on our long family journey.

Somewhere in the period of 1300 AD, our family was most likely in Switzerland. I will supply information on the Anabaptist Mennonite farmers in that time period, which includes the Knusli family in the area around Zurich, Switzerland. Our ancestors were farmers of the highest order for centuries and in some cases still are today. Our ancestors were persecuted for their Mennonite religious beliefs and this persecution eventually drove many of our family members to America for the goal of religious freedom and freedom from persecution. Different branches moved at different times in the early 1700's. Some of the branches remained behind and are still located in the area of Switzerland located near Zurich and Eggiwill. I will try to detail as much as I can of the different branches and their journeys in this book.

There are many histories of our family members and I have included as many as I have been able to locate, so you will have an understanding not only where they came from but also who they were, and what they accomplished and sacrificed along the way.

I hope you enjoy reading the history of our family based on the 15 years of my research work.

Introduction

This book covers many centuries of the history of the Knusli family. It began rather simply in Eastern section of Africa in the Rift Valley, perhaps in present day Ethiopia, Kenya, or Tanzania some 31,000 to 79,000 years ago, where the common ancestor of every non-African man living today originated. Scientists put the most likely date at around 50,000 years ago. A group of as few as 10 or as many as 20 individuals left that area in search of food and worked their way north and spread out to populate all corners of the world. This was a very hazardous period in history and we can be thankful that these early pioneers did not end up losing their lives during this journey. The fact that we are alive is the evidence that they were successful in their efforts. I'm sure they did not start out on their journey with any idea that they were going to populate the world. They were simply moving after the animals that supplied their needs. The animals probably led them to water and to other necessities to sustain their lives. As they moved they had children, these children continued to spread out to other locations, and as they moved and stayed in locations for long periods, their bodies began to evolve to reflect the environment in which they lived with my family line eventually reaching the eastern end of the Mediterranean Sea. There were many generations of the family during this period of family history and I'm sure many perished due to the very hazardous conditions they met along the way, but they managed to cover approximately 4,000 miles during the approximate 30,000 years of their travel. Our family line ended up in the area of Anatolia or Levant in what is current day Turkey between 15,000 and 22,000 years ago and then to the Fertile Crescent area about 10,000 years ago. They eventually made it to Zurich Switzerland, then along the Rhine River to the Alsace Province, then to Rotterdam in Netherlands and into England and on to Philadelphia and then to Lancaster PA in America. I will try to give you an idea of what they faced on each of these stops and tell you the stories that my research and the research of other family members has uncovered. I will also give you our direct ancestor line from Zurich, Switzerland to their arrival on a farm located about 1 mile west of Lancaster, PA on the Harrisburg Pike in East Hempfield Township and as they continued to grow and prosper in the United States of America. Our family is now spread throughout the world and there are well over 3,000 different surnames used by direct descendants of Hans Knussli, who was born in Switzerland in 1628. The number of surnames is probably much larger than that, since I have not been able to track down all the descendants on all the branches of the family tree. I continue to work on our family line and will continue to connect as many members of the family as I can find and develop. I recently was contacted by a Knisely descendant whose ancestor came to America in 1739, 22 years after our direct line arrived. DNA testing on one of their male family members confirmed a relationship. Their ancestor came from Berne, Switzerland and our ancestor Hans Knussli lived in that area for many years. There is most likely a family link in that area, but to date no link has been found.

CHAPTER ONE

DNA and Genealogy

When you say the word Genealogy, the Gene in Genealogy refers to DNA, thus they are considered one and the same. Genealogists tend to center their efforts on building a paper trail of their family, but DNA testing can assist in helping to build a paper trail. The DNA information in my case was the result of Jake Knisely and I submitting samples to Family Tree DNA, and the information they returned to me gave me a explanation that our Y-DNA was in a J2 Haplogroup. This led me to research the J2 Haplogroup classification on the internet and I found information pointing to the area of Mesopotamia and the roots of our family which indicated we were part of the first group 10,000 years ago who moved away from hunting and gathering and began learning to farm the land by using irrigation and also domesticating animals to assist in the work of farming.

Later on, I was asked to allow a group in Greece to add my Y-DNA to a study they were performing on the Haplogroup J2. In order to better define my DNA for this study, I had a Deep Clade test completed on my DNA which allowed the study to use this information to indicate that I was a descendant of a common man who lived 15,000 to 22,000 years ago in the general area of Anatolia or Levant in present day Turkey. I also updated my Y-DNA test to 37 markers which helped the J2 study to better place my DNA. This test also supplied the evolutionary changes that had occurred in my DNA during the last 50,000 years and placed my DNA in the J2b2 haplogroup. Later I submitted my Y-DNA information to the National Geographic Genographic Project and they supplied me with additional information on the journey my ancestors took. This along with the book and DVD "Journey of Man" by Dr. Spencer Wells allowed me more insight into what the Y-DNA results were showing. DNA is a complicated subject matter and since I am a neophyte at DNA, I will try to keep it simple. I know you do not want to read a lot of information that will be difficult to understand. DNA is a part of our very core and it has been likened to a Time Travel Machine that is equipped with a tape recorder. It also needs to be noted that 99.9% of our DNA is the same for the total current population of the world. The 0.1% is the difference that is responsible for our individual traits, eye color, risk for health problems, etc. for example and some of it means nothing at all at this time. If you are a male, your core Y-DNA came from all of your direct line male ancestors and part of your DNA came from the male individuals who lived about 50,000 years ago in Eastern Africa. Every 4,000 to 5,000 years of living in an area creates the opportunity for the bodies of the descendants to begin to evolve or mutate into what would be the best fit of their genes that will adapt their bodies to the area in which they are living. The best example I can supply of this type of evolution is the Alaskan Eskimo's bodies have evolved to longer bodies and shorter extremities in order to keep their hands and feet closer to the main source of heat in the body. This is not a quick change but rather a slowly developing evolution that takes many generations to evolve. In a period, covering 5,000 years there would be between 200 to 250 family generations to accomplish an evolutionary change. These changes can be found in the recorded information in your DNA and will assist in supplying information on the journey that your family took. The mutations are passed down from the individual whose body generated this mutation and if your DNA matches with another person, it indicates a relationship link to that person. If your surname also matches that person there is a good possibility you will be able to establish a paper trail,

I should point out that the female DNA is called Mitochondrial DNA referred to as mtDNA and traces the female DNA back through the chain of mother to mother to mother, so a Knusli female have a different path than the path of her father and brothers. I should also point out that the male body also has the mtDNA of his mother and a test can be performed on this portion of his DNA to determine the path his mother and her ancestors took in traveling through the last 50,000 years.

The DNA tests I undertook connected me to Jake Knisely, who also submitted a sample and since he had a paper trail history going back to the year 1628, it allowed me the surety that there was a link in his data that would be my paper trail back to Hans Knussli and the Knusli name, which was a Zurich, Switzerland surname. It took several years and the assistance of some other researchers to locate the link that we needed to connect. For those of you who are doing your own research on a different male surname line, there may be help in the DNA testing procedure that could result in a quantum leap in your research. The DNA test is a simple swab of your cheek and is totally painless and the cost has been falling rapidly during the last few years. I should caution you that not all tests result in the type of results I achieved with my DNA. Utilizing all of this technology, I was able to construct a relatively accurate picture of our family journey.

In the next chapter, I will begin to define the journey that carried us from the beginning to the current day which will be a journey of around 50,000 years and over 10,000 miles from Eastern Africa to Lancaster, PA in 1717 and our family spread from there to all over the US and Canada. We are a very large family and we have moved to all the different corners of the world. The journey we made was a stop and go journey through time with almost impossible odds that the journey would deliver us to the present day. With all of the elements that might have killed off our ancestors it is a miracle of God that we made it through this journey. As I tell of our long journey, I will be including the world history and the history our ancestors experienced as they traveled through the portions of the time in which they lived.

CHAPTER TWO

In The Beginning

Worldwide DNA testing, by Dr. Spencer Wells, has indicated that our ancestors began their journey approximately 50,000 years ago in the Eastern area of Africa. This was in the region of the Rift Valley somewhere around Ethiopia, Kenya, or Tanzania. The individuals currently living in this area today have the evolutionary factor identified as M168 in their DNA and they lack the other evolutionary factors that exist in individuals currently living in other parts of the world. The M168 factor was the first common genetic factor found in all of the non-African widespread members in the world and indicates that we all evolved from our original ancestors who began their life in this area of Africa. They were among the first of the Homo sapiens that would eventually spread throughout the world. So what did these individuals look like? They were dark skinned due to living in an area where there was a large number of sunny days. There is Melanin in our skin that works by darkening our skin to provide protection from receiving excessive amounts of Vitamin D. The further north or south that you move from the equator, evolution will cause the skin to become lighter. This is not a quick change but rather a gradual change through evolution and takes thousands of years to occur. These individuals were most likely similar to us in many other ways. Since they lived in a warm climate, it was unlikely that they had a lot of heavy body hair to help protect them from the cold. They were most likely near the same height as we are, give or take some deviation just as there is in our current day population. They were using stone tools and there is evidence of early art and advance conceptual skills.

They were living in a period of time when there was a temporary retreat of the ice age causing Africa's desert climate to move from drought to warmer temperatures and moister conditions. These conditions would have allowed this group of people to begin their journey to the north. They were skilled at hunting and gathering and depended on the animals and plants to sustain themselves and the weather conditions would have allowed the animals to begin moving in a northern direction. The melting of the ice as it moved back up into Europe would have changed the drought in the deserts to nice grassland along with some natural lakes that would be favorable for the animals. Our ancestors would just naturally have followed the animals as they moved. This increased vegetation would also have been helpful to them for food and would have made it easier for them to hunt the animals, by hiding in the higher grasses. Since our ancestors were nomadic they would have followed as the animals moved and while it is not known the exact path they followed, speculation is that they would have followed the coast or waterways, which would have provided both the animals and our ancestors with a good supply of water which was necessary for their survival.. The African Rift Valley is part of a massive line of upheaval formed by the movement of great tectonic plates of the earth's crust and as a result created a string of lakes running along it's length. The Red Sea is also part of the Rift Valley and would have helped provide water for their journey. Some believe they stayed to the west of the Red Sea and moved eastward around the top and on up to the east of the Mediterranean Sea. However, research seems to confirm that water levels being low from the Ice Age would have allowed them to cross at the southern end of the Red Sea, where the water level would have been very shallow and allowed them to use primitive boats or to just wade across, as is shown on the map on the next page. Either path would have provided a good path northward for both the animals and our ancestors, allowing them to move but remain near water.

Along about the same time as this movement north there seemed to be a leap forward in intellectual capacity. There is archaeological evidence of stone tools, early art and advanced conceptual skills. The emergence of language gave them a huge advantage over other early human species. Improved tools and weapons, the ability to plan and learning to cooperate with one another and an increased capacity to utilize resources in new ways allowed modern humans the ability to move to new regions and utilize the new and available resources.

This map shows the approximate path of the journey of the J2 Haplogroup including the evolutionary factors in our DNA. This

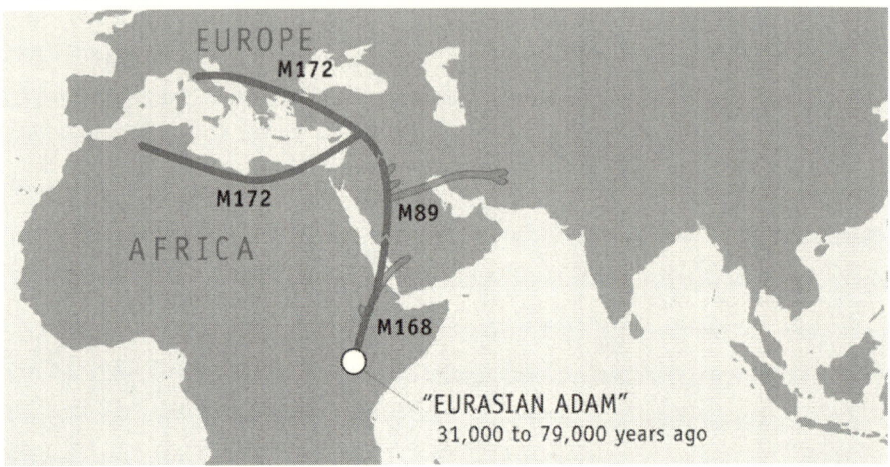

path shows the trip as east of the Red Sea used by the early DNA ancestors of the Knusli family to move out of Africa. This map is taken from the National Geographic Genographic Project.

The move through Africa to the north consumed as many as 30,000 years of our total journey and there were approximately 800 to 1,300 generations of our family tree created during this journey that began with a small group of 10 to 20 individuals. Our family group continued to move towards the eastern end of the Mediterranean Sea. Other groups began to separate and spread out to other parts of the world during this northern journey. Many of these other groups that headed off in an easterly direction would eventually populate many different sections of the world. Some of this north eastern movement was made possible by the Ice Age which caused sea levels to decline and exposed some underwater land bridges that allowed travel to areas on foot that would not be available under current ocean levels. Our family evolved and established an evolutionary factor named M89 about 40,000 to 45,000 years ago as we branched off in a northern direction towards the eastern end of the Mediterranean Sea. Eventually somewhere in this 10,000 to 22,000 year period of time we developed a new evolutionary factor named M172 that occurred in an area north of the eastern end of the Mediterranean Sea.

The next Chapter will cover the growth and events in our ancestor's journey during the period of time they lived in the area around the eastern end of the Mediterranean Sea

CHAPTER THREE

Mediterranean Sea Area

Our family spent a long time moving around this area on their journey through time. They arrived in this area around 22,000 BC and began to spread out over this entire area and eventually continued their trek across the continent north of the Mediterranean Sea and into Switzerland and arrived there around the year 1300 AD. Since there are no other major mutations or evolutionary changes evident in our DNA analysis, it is assumed that we were not in the Switzerland area until somewhere around 1300 AD. As you will read in a later chapter, there is more justification for the date of 1300 AD. I also based this on the assumption that an evolutionary change would normally take place at approximately 4,000 to 5,000 years of living in a specific area, a sort of environmental adjustment to the area. Our J2 family probably spent around 19,000 to 22,000 years moving around the area north, east and south of the Mediterranean Sea area. Because of the higher volume of history available for this area, I will cover several different places in this region and some of the history for these areas. There is archeology information available that indicates that DNA from the J2 haplogroup was located in many different places in the Mediterranean region. It is hard to be sure at this point in time if it was our ancestors or just relatives of our ancestors whose DNA was found in these areas, although many of our ancestors, perhaps as many as 700 to 800 generations, lived and died in this area during the period of time they resided here and some of our ancestors may well have been in all of these areas at different times.

Anatolia Region

Our DNA had a mutation in this area and developed a factor in our DNA identified as M172 around 20,000 - 13,000 BC. This individual became the father of the many widely scattered and diverse lines of the J haplogroup. He was a descendant of the M89 mutation or evolutionary factor from the Middle Eastern Africa Clan. At the period of time they were in this area, they were hunters and gatherers and were cave dwellers in this area. This was the period in time called the Paleolithic period and there are many caves and human remains. The human remains that have been discovered are where they found the DNA evidence confirming our presence in Anatolia. Time dating of the remains gave them the period of the beginning of our Haplogroup J. There were also evidence of animal bones and fruits found in this area. There are caves containing paintings that go back for as many as 250,000 years. This area was a strategic location of the intersection of Asia and Europe and was a center of several civilizations since prehistoric times. Many of our DNA relatives still live in this area but it is also inhabited by many other people from other regions.

Our Y-DNA relatives moved out of this area in many different directions all around the Mediterranean Sea, north, east and south. The Anatolian region was the area between the Mediterranean Sea to the south and the Black Sea to the north, with the Aegean Sea to the west, which is the location of current day Turkey.

It was in this area where the male skull developed a small rounded bump on the base of the skull where the spine enters the skull. This bump was given the name of the Anatolia bump and the male Knusli descendants I have checked all have this same bump on their skull. It feels like a small round ball right in the center bottom of the skull above where the spine enters the skull. You do not have to be a Knusli descendant to have the bump since any of the early descendants of this area will have the bump. It is a distinct DNA feature of people from this area.

Fertile Crescent Region

Members of the J Haplogroup moved into the Fertile Crescent region during the period of 12,000 - 2800 BC. The Knusli Haplogroup is defined as J2b2 and research tells us that this mutation that developed the J2 Haplogroup originated in the northern part of the Fertile Crescent area where it later spread throughout central Asia, the Mediterranean, south into India and towards Europe. The Knusli family's ancestors were part of two groups who left this area and eventually moved toward Europe with the other large group who left this area who were most likely Hebrews from Abraham's family line. The Fertile Crescent is a region that extends from the Mediterranean Sea to the Persian Gulf where the Euphrates and Tigris Rivers run. This land contained very rich soil that was suited for the eventual development of excellent farming of crops. Currently it is believed that this is where a major change took place in the development of families. The lack of animals to hunt and a thinning of natural crops began to restrict the people's ability to support their families, who were still practicing hunting and gathering as a way of feeding themselves. They were living in caves at this time and as the ability to supply the need for food dwindled, they began to move out of the caves and down towards the lakes and rivers in this area. Around 10,000 BC, they began to develop the skills required to raise their own crops for food and to develop excellent farming techniques to produce large crops capable of supporting the growing number of extended family members. One of the developments was a method of irrigation to water their crops. This development was big breakthrough that allowed for larger and better crops that included crops of tall, wild grasses, including an early type of barley, and primitive varieties of wheat called emmer and einkorn. These naturally produced large grains (seeds) that were tasty and nourishing. This allowed for the beginning of families supporting themselves and staying in one location giving them the opportunity to expand their families and start developing communities. This period also led to the domestication or training of animals to help them perform the tasks involved in farming the land. By around 9000 BC, they were storing grains during the winter, then sowing them in specially cleared plots in the spring. By 8000 BC, the farmers had discovered which grains gave the best yields and selected these for planting. They produced more food than they needed and were able to feed non-farmers such as craft workers and traders. The farmers then exchanged their food for various kinds of useful or decorative goods. It was in this area around 3500 BC, that the wheel was invented, followed closely by the cart that could be pulled by the tamed animals to assist them in their farm work. It also led to wider and quicker travel carrying people and supplies around the region, thus spreading the families and goods to wider and wider circles of civilization. This small region became the area where many different civilizations developed. The first known of these civilizations were the Sumerians, they were replaced in turn by the Assyrians and then by the Babylonians. Today this land is known as Iraq. Later on the Greeks called this area Mesopotamia, which means "between the rivers".

The earliest known civilization of the Fertile Crescent were the Sumerians who lived in this area beginning around 2900 - 1800 BC, where they lived in the southern section of the Mesopotamia region in a number of independent cities or states with names such as Ur, Lagash, and Eridu, to name a few. The rulers of these city-states were constantly at war with one another, with the wars leading to the growth of larger cities as the more powerful cities swallowed up the smaller cities. Most of these wars were fought over water which was a scarce and valuable resource in this area. The war tactic used in many instances was to surround the city and trap everyone inside. Over time, the residents of the city began to starve to death and then it was easy to take control of the city. These cities were often rectangular, surrounded by high, wide walls and inside the gates were broad avenues used for religious processions or victory parades. The largest buildings were called ziggurats, pyramid like temples that soared toward the heavens and on the top stood a shrine to the chief god or goddess of the city. Their sloping sides had terraces, or wide steps, that were sometimes planted with trees and shrubs. The language they spoke was unlike any other human language that is known today and they began to write and record information on the Sumerian culture of religion, government structure, literature and their laws. They developed what appears to be the world's first system of monarchy which was ruled by a priest-king who controlled the military, trade, settling disputes, and was the leader of the important religious ceremonies. These priest-kings ruled through a series of bureaucrats that were mostly priests that assigned land and distributed crops after they were harvested. Much of this was recorded on wet clay blocks which would then dry into stone hard tablets which survived these many years and still tell the stories of what happened during that period.

The careful planning of the harvest required them to develop methods of measuring and recording time. As a result, they developed a calendar containing 12 months based on the cycle of the moon. This calendar method required a leap month every three years to catch up with the sun. With the planning now organized, they needed a method of counting what was being done. So they developed what was the first mathematics that was used by humans.

They believed in and worshipped many Gods, who resembled humans and were creator Gods who had created the world and the people who lived in it. They had a belief that the Gods regretted creating humans and sent a flood to destroy their creations but one man survived by building a boat. Ur, one of these Sumerian cities, is mentioned in Genesis as the home of Abram, son of Terah, who became the patriarch Abraham, the originator of the Hebrew religion. He was also the ancestor of Jesus, so this also leads us to the possibility that Jesus was a relative of our family. Jesus's ancestry is listed in the Bible and while there are several different versions of his direct ancestral line, they all lead back to Abraham through David.

Genesis 11:31

Terah took his son Abram, his grandson Lot, son of Haran, and his daughter-in-law Sarai, the wife of his son Abram, and together they set out from Ur of the Chaldeans to go to Canaan. But when they came to Haran, they settled there.

DNA research tells us that the Haplogroup J2 counts approximately 30% of its members as people who are members of the Hebrew religion and these J2 individuals would have a high probability of being at least DNA relatives of ours. This is an additional indication of our family's presence in this area and period. It should also be noted that currently there are three individuals who are members of the Hebrew or Jewish religion that have a 100% 12 marker Y-DNA match to me even though their last names are different than mine. One of these individuals contacted me, studied both of our DNA markers, and estimated that we were in the area of 30th cousins. One major difference in our Y-DNA markers was in the Cohan Marker where we had a difference of 3 points. His value indicated an Abraham descendant and mine did not. This would confirm the probability that people who are descendants of Abraham would be distant relatives to our family. I was also told that members of the Hebrew faith did not start using surnames until 1600 AD, which could have placed them as relatives of our Knusli line that may have branched off to another section of Europe when our ancestors moved into Switzerland.

Many inventions were created in this period and in this region. One of the most far reaching of the Sumerians inventions was the law. Their law was written and administered by a centralized authority. It required the individual to take the accused into court with the court determining the punishment or penalty to be exacted. The law they developed was a law of exact revenge, a kind of "an eye for an eye, a tooth for a tooth, and a life for a life".

It is impossible to know what part our ancestors or our relatives may have played in all of this, but with our history being farmers for the most part, we were probably part of the development of the farming methods that spread from this area to the rest of the world.

Jericho

The biblical town of Jericho or as it was called in the early years, Tell el-Sultan, is located a short distance from the current city of Jericho. Our ancestors or relatives left a physical footprint in this town on their genetic journey. There was settlement and artifacts indicating permanent human settlement dating as far back as 11,000 years. It was about 1200 BC, when the walls came tumbling down. There is archeology research that indicates the original walls were brought down by some force instead of crumpling of age. The Bible tells us that Joshua after leading the Israelites across the Jordan went to the city of Jericho and was instructed by God to march around the city once every day for six days with the priests carrying their rams horns. On the seventh day, they were to walk around the city seven times and then blow their rams horns. Once they blew their horns, the walls collapsed and they were able to invade the city and conquer the entire city. All the occupants were killed except for Rahab and her family. She was spared because she hid two of Joshua's spies. The entire city was laid to waste and burned and Joshua put a jinx on anyone who would rebuild the city. It was 400 years before it was rebuilt. Someone jokingly asked if our ancestors were inside or outside the walls. Jake Knisely's tongue in cheek answer was that since we are alive our ancestors were outside the walls, since everyone inside was killed. However, we do not specifically know if it was our ancestors or our relatives that were in the area of Jericho. It would, at the very least, have been some of our J2 haplogroup cousins, since there were samples of our J2 haplogroup Y-DNA located in this area.

When you consider all the things that occurred here and in all the years that followed, with the dangers that were inherit with the wars, the droughts, the diseases, famines, the natural disasters of earthquakes, tornadoes, hurricanes, floods, and volcanoes, it is a miracle of God, as I mentioned earlier, that we are alive today. The fact that we are alive is the result of one man living long enough to father a male, who in turn fathered a male, etc. for over 2,300 generations. The odds of this happening are astronomical. We should all be thankful for just being alive today, since one death anywhere along this chain of our ancestral path would have ended our line.

The next section of our family journey was in the movement of our ancestors from the Fertile Crescent area into Europe in the area of Zurich, Switzerland. This long journey covered many miles and took many years.

CHAPTER FOUR

Journey to Zurich

The journey from the Fertile Crescent area to Zurich, Switzerland covered around 2,275 miles and while it is impossible to be sure when our ancestors left the Fertile Crescent area, it was such a long journey, that I assume it would have taken a long period of time, perhaps as long as 2,600 years or maybe even longer to travel this section of the journey. While we are not sure of the time of the movement, we will assume they left the Fertile Crescent area sometime after 1300 BC and arrived in the area of Zurich, Switzerland sometime after 1300 AD. As you will read later, there is more justification for the estimate on their arrival in Switzerland. This was a stop and go trip since they would most likely have settled in an area, established a home and raised a family and as the

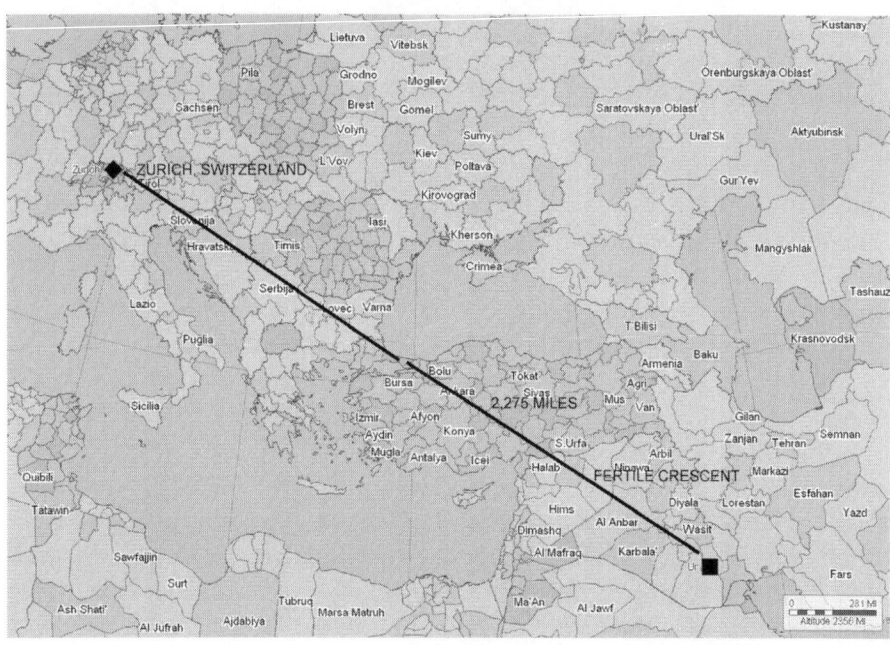

Nussli Journey
Fertile Crescent to Zurich Switzerland

family grew some of the family members, our ancestors, would have continued to move westward and repeated that same process many different times before reaching Switzerland. There were most likely 50 to 130 generations of our family involved in the movement towards Switzerland. In addition to moving westward, some family members would have also spread out in different directions, but our direct line ancestors would have continued to move towards Switzerland. The most likely route is shown in the map on the previous page, since this route would have been the most direct land route from the Fertile Crescent area through to Europe and would have passed through the area of present day Istanbul, located southeast of the Black Sea. History reports that during this period, when our ancestors would have passed through this area, there were indications of some small settlements there around 512 BC and then in 313 AD the area came under control of the Roman Empire and was named "New Rome". It was later named Constantinople to honor the latest Roman Emperor Constantine. Many years later in 1261 AD, the city was captured back from the Romans and the city's name was then changed to Istanbul.

The area around present day Istanbul was a very busy trade route for both land and sea since it was close to the Mediterranean Sea and was located on a land mass between it and the Black Sea and that allowed land travel into Europe. This would have created a meeting place and travel route for many traders and merchants coming from and going to Europe with goods. This is why I suspect that our family traveled through this area. They should have reached this area somewhere around 300 BC to 300 AD. It would be a halfway point between the start and end of this section of their journey. This area was under the control of the Roman Empire by the time they went through this area. In fact, the Roman Empire controlled all of the land from the Fertile Crescent area to Zurich, Switzerland at the height of its reign. It is almost a certainty that our family lived in different areas along this route when it was controlled by the Roman Empire from the time shortly before the birth of Jesus until approximately 400 years after his death. So when you read about the history of the Roman Empire, you will now be aware that our ancestors and relatives of our ancestors were subjects of the Roman Empire. It also should help you to understand how fortunate we are that these ancestors survived this period with all the battles that were fought throughout the reign of the Roman Empire. It is difficult to imagine the difficulties they met during this period.

The next stop on the journey would be in Switzerland, where members of our family are still living today. In fact, there could still be relatives of our direct family still living in areas all along this route from the Middle East to Switzerland but their names would be different from ours and tough to identify as members of our family. Some would match our DNA and it is possible that some of them at some time will take a test. If that occurs and they use Family Tree DNA for the test, I will be notified of the match. At the current time, there are a large number of Knusli surnames in the Zurich telephone directory. DNA testing would most likely confirm that they are cousins of our family.

The next leg of our ancestor's journey would lead us over the Alps mountain range. It was a foreboding obstacle to overcome to reach Switzerland. Climbing over the mountain range meant traveling over 200 miles of up and down mountains many times to move from the Italian side into Zurich completing another hazardous section of travel.

CHAPTER FIVE

<u>Zurich Switzerland</u>

Switzerland in the early years was populated by a group of people named Helvetians and the name Helvetia became the name for the area that later became known as Switzerland. The Helvetians were a Celtic Tribe, from the area of England, and had moved into Switzerland in the period between 500 BC and 400 AD. They were considered a barbaric tribe of people by the Greeks and Romans, although this is questionable, since they were skilled craftsmen and were highly skilled in the working of metal. Their carts and wagons were superior to even the ones made by the Romans. Their name today lives on in the Latin name of Helvetia for Switzerland. The CH seen on Swiss train cars and on their internet domain stands for Confoederatio Helvetica which is the Latin version of Swiss Confederation. The Nusli family line that came out of Switzerland and eventually moved to Lancaster, PA in 1717, at the same time as the Knusli family line, has been DNA tested as R1b1, which would indicate that they were most likely descendants of the original Celtic Tribes. This also confirms that they are a separate family line.

On August 1, 1291, there was a reorganization of Helvetica and it became known as the Old Swiss Confederation. One of the developments of this period was the opening of a new transalpine trading route that opened up 3 small valleys in Central Switzerland. The opening of this route allowed easier passage for new traffic to the area from Italy and the Mediterranean Sea. Since our family would have been coming from the Mediterranean Sea area, I would suggest that this route opened up a passage for our ancestors to move into Switzerland. Although we may never know for certain when they arrived in Switzerland, these two pieces of information establish a basis for indicating that our ancestors most likely moved into Switzerland in circa 1300 AD. Since the Knusli surname is said to originate in the Zurich Switzerland area it would indicate that our ancestors moved to Zurich after they came over the mountain.

Hans Knussli was born in the Canton of Zurick in Switzerland in 1628. I have information on other Knusli members who were born in this area prior to Hans, but no connection at the current time has linked any of these Knusli members to our ancestor Hans. If you look at Appendix G, you will find a list of Knusli and Knussli names who at this time are not connected to our line. However, it is likely all of these people would be relatives and some might be our ancestors. We continue to look for these links.

The Black Plague

Between the arrival of our family in Switzerland and the birth of Hans Knussli 1628, there was another threat to the continuation of our ancestors. In 1348, the Black Plague arrived in Europe and it spread widely through the different countries. In Bern, Switzerland, they were burying as many as 60 bodies per day, due to deaths from the disease. This rapidly advancing disease came in two forms:

The Pneumonic Plague that caused fever and the spitting up of blood along with small black pustules on the body and it was given the name, The Black Death. This was the most infectious form and was usually fatal. People who were infected became bed ridden for 2 to 3 days and died by the 3rd or 4th day.

The Bubonic Plague was spread by fleas, and the symptoms were fever and carbuncles and enlarged lymph glands or buboes as they were called and resulted in this ailment being named the bubonic plague. The recovery rate for this ailment was much higher than the other type.

Once the death rate reached around 70% of the population in an area, the remaining survivors were probably immune and tended to survive. Switzerland's population declined from around 800,000 in 1300 AD to 600,000 in 1400 AD as a direct result of the Black Plague. It is likely some of our ancestors relatives died during this period, but our direct line ancestors were able to make it and survive.

The 1500's in Switzerland

As I mentioned above, I have located several Knusli individuals in the Zurich Switzerland area. The earliest was a Jagli or Jacob Knusli, who was born circa 1557. I have not been able to connect him to our family but having the same surname, he is most likely an ancestor or a relative of our line. I have also been able to locate over 30 Knusli individuals that were born between 1557 and 1654. Hopefully someday we will find a link to these individuals.

The two major areas for the Knusli family were the Canton of Zurich and then later the Canton of Bern. Our family name, as I mentioned before, was noted as originating in the Zurich area. Our family joined with the Anabaptist group sometime after this group started in 1520. At the current time, there is no record of when they became part of this group. The persecution in Zurich increased during the 1640's and by that time, the Anabaptist groups began calling themselves Anabaptist Mennonites. The persecution in that area increased and Hans Knussli, our direct ancestor, along with his parents or perhaps by himself, was forced to move to Zell in the Canton of Bern in circa 1647. They lived there until circa 1671, at which time they were again forced to leave this area and move to the Alsace Province. There were others of his family line who lived in this area and later on a member of that group and his family moved to America in 1739. I will cover more of this line later in the book.

There were thirteen sovereign cantons in the Old Swiss Confederation and they each had their own constitution, legislature, government, and courts. The city of Zurich was located in the Canton of Zurich, which was one of the thirteen Cantons. The map that follows shows the original Canton of Zurich and the twelve districts that make up the Canton.

Anabaptist Mennonites in Switzerland

In the early beginnings of the Mennonite religion, they were known simply as Anabaptists or in German as "Taufer", which meant Baptists. They were part of the large group that separated from the practices of the Roman Catholic Church which was established in Switzerland during the time the Romans were in control of this area. This separation was referred to as the Protestant Reformation. The most prominent feature of Anabaptist separation centered on infant baptism which had both religious and political meaning, since almost every child born in Western Europe was baptized at birth by the Roman Catholic Church. The Anabaptists also had significant theological views that differed from other Protestant reformers like Martin Luther and Huldrych (Ulrich) Zwingli. All the groups held a belief that the church should be separate from the government, but the Mennonites held the belief that people should become members of the church only after they professed their belief in Jesus. This excluded children from joining and being baptized until they reached an age of knowledge to express their beliefs. On January 21, 1525, fifteen men gathered to baptize each other, including Conrad Grebel, Felix Manz, and George Blaurock, who were the early leaders of this movement in Zurich. This marked the official separation of the Anabaptist Movement in Europe. They were strongly opposed by Zwingli, founder of the Reformed Church, and other authorities, but their convictions were rapidly spreading in the villages around Zurich. Their message struck a strong chord with the peasants, who had become upset with the clerical and economic abuses that they were experiencing at the hands of the Catholic Church. The Anabaptists also were strong in the belief of anti-violence. Zwingli and his Reformed followers would fight to defend themselves and this difference caused part of the problem for the non-violent movement.

During this early period a Catholic Priest, Menno Simons started to rethink his Catholic faith. He had a brother involved in the Anabaptist movement who was killed for his beliefs and was killed when he refused to defend himself. This stemmed from their belief that God did not condone killing or the use of force for any reason even in their own defense. His brother's death changed his thinking about the Catholic Church and in 1536, at the age of 40, Menno chose to leave the Catholic Church and he became a leader in the non-violent Anabaptist movement. A priest leaving the Catholic Church to join an Anabaptist Movement in that time violated a sacred trust and as a result, he became a hunted man with a price on his head for the rest of his life. His first name, Menno, became associated with the scattered groups of non-violent Anabaptists around Europe, that eventually adopted the name of Mennonites and the name spread all over the world as the religion grew in size and members. Later on, a group separated from the Mennonites because of a difference in the frequency of communion. A young Swiss elder named Jakob Ammann began to suggest some changes and this led to a series of meetings over a long period of time, after which Ammann decided to separate from the Mennonites and organized a new group that took the name Amish. Part of this separation was the difference in the handling of sinners. The Mennonites believed in trying to bring the shunned sinners back into the fold whereas the Amish felt they should not be allowed to return.

Hans Knussli's Family in Switzerland

Our ancestors became part of this non-violent group of Anabaptists sometime in the early beginnings of this new religion. Although we do not know the name of the first ancestor to join this group, it was most likely one of Hans Knussli's ancestors who joined this group early in the development of this religious movement that took place in Switzerland. Hans was our First Generation ancestor where we have a name assigned to him and descendants that we know are our ancestors.

Our ancestor Hans Knussli was born on October 11, 1628 in the Canton of Zurick in Switzerland and died around 1688 in Alsace Province between France and the Rhine River. He was married three times. He was forced to move, perhaps along with his parents, to Eggiwil, Canton of Bern, Switzerland sometime prior to 1648.

Barbara Agerter was his first wife. They were married in 1648 and she bore him one son Johannes Hans Knussli born December 9, 1649. She died while delivering her child and her son, Johannes stayed in Eggiwil when his father was forced to leave Eggiwil. Hans' second wife was Elsbeth Muller. They were married on January 11, 1650 in Eggiwil. They had five children, George, Barbali (who died young), Antonius Kristopher (our direct ancestor), a second Barbali, and Anna. Of these children, all of them except Antonius Kristopher stayed in Switzerland. Hans' third wife was Cathri Wermuth, who he married in Alsace Province on October 22, 1688. They did not have any children. It is thought Hans and Cathri died while they were in Alsace Province.

Hans Knussli and his son Antonius Kristopher moved from Eggiwil, most likely by foot, for around 70 miles to Basil where they could have used a raft to go down the Rhine River to Alsace, between Germany and France to escape the persecution that they had faced in Eggiwil. My research uncovered information that these people were forced to leave Eggiwil with just the belongings they could carry and then by boat or raft on the river. The Rhine River tributaries flow all the way from the Alps through Zurich and then Basil and then through the Rhine Valley of Germany and on to Rotterdam in the Netherlands. If you have the opportunity to take the Rhine River cruise by ship from Basil that ends in Rotterdam, you will be traveling on this same journey. The Alsace Province was a large area located along the western bank of the Rhine River between France and Germany which were separated by the Rhine River. Alsace Province and a large section of France and Germany was the place where many Anabaptist were slaughtered during the period of the Thirty Year War. The village of Ensisheim in this area was named "the slaughterhouse of Alsace," since six hundred Anabaptists were killed there within a few years. After the war ended in 1648 the Mennonites and some other Anabaptist groups were invited to move back into the area due to a change in policy on the part of the government. A small group of Mennonite families moved to this area somewhere around 1650, with a much larger group moving from Switzerland in 1671, which included a group of seven hundred who were exiled from the Canton of Bern, who began to arrive in Alsace. They were sent there without any of their personal belongings, some on wagons overland and some by boat downstream. They arrived sick and poor without the majority of their possessions. They were also stripped of their Swiss citizenship when they were exiled. There is no record of exactly when our ancestor Hans and his son Antonius moved to Alsace but we do know Hans died in Alsace around 1688 and Antonius married his wife in 1677 in Alsace so it is an assumption that they moved there with the group in 1671.

It should also be noted there were other Knussli relatives who were living in the Berne area and apparently did not move away. They may have hid their Mennonite connection or left the religion to prevent being forced to move. In 1739, a member of this branch of the Knussli family moved to America and settled in York County, Pennsylvania. In 2011, I was able to have a male member of this line test his Y-DNA and his was a perfect match to me and the other members of our line. This connected them as relatives with a common link in Switzerland, however we do not have information how they are linked at this time. Perhaps in the future that connection will be made.

Religious Persecution in Switzerland

During the 125 year period beginning in 1525 when our family joined the Anabaptist Movement and around 1647 when they eventually left the Canton of Zurich, the persecution of the non-violent Anabaptists took many forms. Anabaptism was made a capital crime by the Catholic Church and they made it a crime to feed them or to assist them in any manner. Even some who recanted their religious beliefs were killed. The non-violent group was growing so fast that it caused concern among the other groups in the Reformation. During the time of the Reformation, there were two basic groups involved in the struggles taking place against the Catholic Church. The government was in control of the Catholics and the abuse of the government through the Catholic Church was instrumental in people pushing to separate government and religion. The one group was named Protestants and they joined with the struggles of Martin Luther against what he considered unfair actions by the Pope. Some of the Princes of the area joined Luther's group in the fight and they supported this opposition by fighting. This battle became so severe that it became known as the Thirty Year War and spread all over Europe, and continued to rage until a treaty was established in 1648. This treaty established tolerance between the Catholics and the Protestants but it did not include the Anabaptist Mennonites. The decision to exclude the Anabaptist Mennonites may have pushed our ancestors to leave the area fearing worse persecution. After the treaty there were four religious groups in the Protestant category, the Lutherans (Martin Luther's group), the Reformed (Ulrich Zwingli's group), the Presbyterians, and the Episcopalians.

The other group was the Anabaptists, who later became known as Mennonites, and then the Amish, who were a group that split off the Mennonite group. These two non-violent groups took the worse and most severe punishment because of their anti- violent teachings. They would not fight to defend themselves and in spite of the punishment by the Catholics, they would not give up their beliefs which were part of their Confession of Faith. They believed in no baptism until after a confession of faith, a strong commitment to non-violence, total separation of church and government, a holy life, and some other tenants which were included in their Confession of Faith.

The persecution took many forms over the 120 plus years of the Reformation. Quite a large number of Anabaptists were burned at the stake including a man named Rudolph Lorenz Eisley, whose surname is thought to be a variation of our surname, who was burned at the stake in 1539. It is not likely he was related, but there is the remote possibility that he may have been. Many other leaders were burned at the stake, but it did not seem to deter the growth of their religion. The persecution in other parts of Europe was even more severe than in Switzerland. Other methods of persecution included beheadings, drowning in the Limmat River in Zurich (there is a plague marking this spot a short distance from the train station), random killings by roving bands of soldiers, imprisonment in the Ottenbach Jail, which was close to the Grossmunster Cathedral in Zurich, being placed in ships to row until they died, and other forms of harassment. Imprisonment normally led to an execution when they were released.

If they were found in a home, the home was burned often with them still inside. They were often executed in secret to avoid offending the public. The persecution of the Mennonites exceeded the persecution of the early Christians by Pagan Rome. In order to avoid being discovered, they began to hold their services secretly in their homes and in remote locations, a practice which some groups continue to this day. The picture below shows the view looking out from the Anabaptist (Tauferhohle) Cave which was a location that was used for years as a church where they held their services. The Nusli family used this cave but there is no record of our Knusli family using it. There are tour groups who still hold the service of communions in this cave for those who visit and wish to partake of the rite. This cave is a short distance to the east of the city of Zurich.

There were also safe houses located around Switzerland that were owned by Christians who tried to hide the Mennonites when danger was near. It often cost the owners of the homes fines for hiding them. One such house still stands today and it gives us some information as to how they would run to a house and upon entering would disappear. The house is the Frankhaus near Trub, Canton of Bern in Switzerland. The beam over the door has a date of 1608 carved in a beam, perhaps indicating the date the home was built. There was a side entrance where the Anabaptist who was fleeing an agent would enter and jump over the entrance and just disappear from view. There was a board mounted on a round beam in the floor that would tilt when stepped on. The person would slide down the board and into a safe area under the floor and the board would swing back into place leaving no sign of the opening below. Underneath the board was a small area where they could hide out until the agent had left the area. There were many such places around Switzerland but most have been changed by remodeling and the tilting floor boards have been removed.

Considering the Black Plague and the later persecution through violence created by the groups who opposed the Anabaptist in Switzerland especially in the area around Zurich, it is very fortunate that our ancestors survived and continued our family line. This is another example of God's grace delivering our family through the valley of the shadow of death.

Our next move was from Bern to Alsace where we have found records of Antonius's family.

CHAPTER SIX

Alsace, France

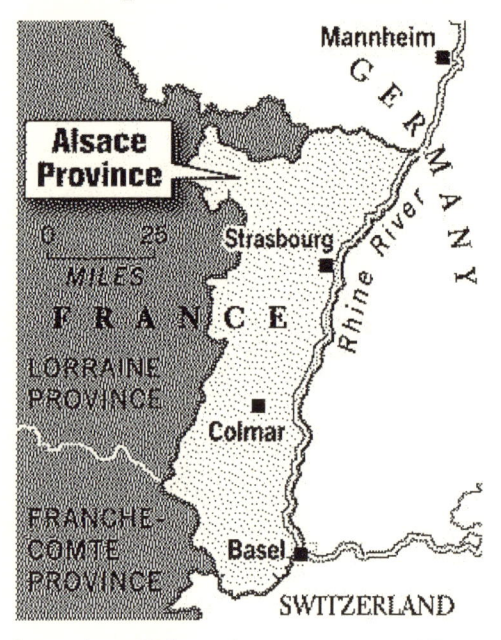

The journey from Eggiwil to Alsace Province as I mentioned earlier was most likely by foot to Basel, Switzerland and then by boat or raft on the Rhine River. There was also the possibility the whole trip could have been made overland by foot or with a wagon. The Palatinate extended from France into Germany on both sides of the Rhine River with Alsace Province located between France and the Rhine River. The earlier severe persecution in Alsace that occurred during the Thirty Year War created a shortage of farmers due to mass murders of Mennonites in that area. As a result, the farm land was laid to waste by the ravages of the war. After the end of the war in 1648, the government in Alsace and in the Palatinate in Germany in general reversed their stance on persecution and began to ask the Mennonites in Switzerland to move to the area with the offer of land they could call their own knowing they would work to improve the land. A few small groups made their way there in 1650 and our ancestor Hans and his son Antonius most likely arrived there by 1671, when the larger groups arrived from Switzerland, which included a group of over 700 who arrived by boats and by wagons. Because of this large influx of Mennonites, the government in 1684 began to offer limited freedom to practice their religion with some restrictions, which included not meeting in public places and no more than 20 in any group meetings. They were also not allowed to entice others to join their religion nor to preach any practices of political revolt and they would also be required to pay a tax to continue to practice their religion. The Mennonites did as they were expected to do and over time the soil recovered and the farms began to prosper. Once this occurred, the government began to push the Mennonites off the land and sell the land to other people.

Antonius's mother Elsbeth Muller had passed away in 1665 and his father Hans was now married to Cathri Wermuth. Cathri, along with George, and sisters Barbali and Anna also made the trip. By 1677, Antonius met and married Magdalena Hempstead and over the next 36 years, they had 11 children. Of these 11 children, only 9 made the trip to America in 1717. There were 2 children, Jacob and Maria, for whom we have no record. They apparently died before 1717, when the family left Alsace to move to America. The other nine children all appeared in the Lancaster area records after their move to America and we have a history on their families. In 1707 a Census was taken in an Unknown location in Alsace. This information was recorded on the website Menno Search operated by Richard Davis. The Census was as follows;

Unknown Alsace Location ca. 1707
Household number 3
Anthoni Knussli, age 52
Magdalena, wife
Hans Kneisly, age 19
Anthony Kneisley, age 14
Elisabeth Kneisley, age 11
Maria Kneisley, age 7
Barbara Kneisley, age 4
Sybilla Kneisley, new born

It is interesting to note that even at this time the spelling of the last name of the children was different than the father's spelling. The first 2 daughters, Anna and Christina, were married before 1707 and were listed with their husbands. Jacob, who was born in circa 1701 apparently died prior to 1707. The last 2 children, George and

Mary were born after 1707. This census confirms where Antonius's family was located in 1707.

In 1707, a group of Mennonites traveled to London, met with William Penn, and arranged terms with him to colonize a portion of what is now Lancaster County in Pennsylvania. In 1709, Hans Herr, John R. Bundely, Martin Meylin (Mylin), Martin Kendig, Jacob Miller, Hans Funk, Hans Graff (Groff), Martin Oberholtzer, and Wendel Bowman bought 10,000 acres of land on the south side of Pequea creek and in 1710 they packed up their families and belongings and made the trip to America and began to work their property.

The Journey to America

This journey began with a boat or raft ride, loaded with their family belongings, down the Rhine River to Rotterdam, Netherlands. The Rhine River flows north from Alsace Province and into Germany and into a large region called the Palatinate, where many Mennonites families moved after the Thirty Years War and then on to Rotterdam where they arranged passage by ship to London, England. Once there, they had to arrange for passage on a ship to the new English colony in America. English ships were the only ships allowed to land in America until after the Revolutionary War. This was not an easy trip and there were many dangers from illness. The length of the trip by ship from Rotterdam to Philadelphia varied due to wind and currents and ranged from seven to twelve weeks.

Following is some information on a journey across the ocean that was recorded in a journal by an Amish passenger, who traveled on the ship Charming Nancy in 1737. The ship our family traveled on was likely to have been slightly smaller than the ship in this 1737 article, so conditions may have been worse.

This information was taken from "Miscellaneous Amish Mennonite Documents," Pennsylvania Mennonite Heritage 2 (July 1979): 12.

"The 28th of June while in Rotterdam (in the Netherlands) getting ready to start my Zernbli died and was buried in Rotterdam. The 29th we got under sail and enjoyed one and a half days of favorable wind. The 7th day of July, early in the morning, Hans Zimmerman's son-in-law died. "

"We landed in England the 8th of July, remaining 9 days in port during which 5 children died. Several days before Michael's Georgli had died."

"On the 29th of July three children died. On the first of August, my Hansli died and the Tuesday previous 5 children died. On the 3rd of August, contrary winds beset the vessel and from the first to the 7th of the month, three more children died. On the 8th of August, Shambien's Lizzie died and on the 9th Hans Zimmerman's Jacobli died. On the 19th, Christian Burgli's child died. Passed a ship on the 21st. A favorable wind sprang up. On the 28th Hans Gasi's wife died. Passed a ship 13th of September."

Landed in Philadelphia on the 18th and my wife and I left ship on the 19th. A child was born to us on the 20th – died – wife recovered. A voyage of 83 days."

The passenger accommodations were open end boxes below deck and the passengers were considered cargo. The people were stored in these boxes feet first and were in there for a long time. Passengers would alternate leaving the boxes to walk in the aisles. I can't even begin to imagine the discomfort they must have experienced.

If you visit the Hans Herr house near Lancaster, you can view the chest that Hans used to store his valuables for the trip. It was a very large chest and would have been very heavy when loaded. They landed in Philadelphia and met with William Penn, who directed them to the property they had purchased. When the group reached their new property in the area of present day Lancaster, they set about building their homes and developing their farms. Many of these farms were located in the area that would later become the center of the town of Lancaster, PA. As they became settled and found the personal and religious freedom they wanted, they began to plan a return trip to encourage more Mennonite families to also come to this area. So in 1717, they sent one of the original members, Hans Kendig, who was by now 70 years old, back to Europe and to the Germany and Alsace areas to encourage others to come to America.

Our Knussli family accepted this invitation and their journey was the same as the original group by following the Rhine River to Rotterdam, in the Netherlands, then by ship to a British port, London, and then by a British ship to Philadelphia in America. This was the typical route of travel for Swiss and German immigrants to America during the early 1700's. They and others by the names of Andreas Kauffman who married Elizabeth Knussli and Isaac Kauffman who married Anna Knussli, Michael Miller who married Barbara Knussli, John Witmer, Hans Shank, Hans Brubaker, Henry Musselman, with their families embracing 363 persons came to Philadelphia a few days before September 8, 1717, where they seem to have been met by Martin Kendig and Hans Herr who conducted them to Lancaster Co, PA (This information was taken from the "Origin of the Kneisley Family" history book). There is a report that indicates large groups of Mennonites were cluttering up the dock in London, so Hans Kendig made a visit to Queen Ann and requested that she fund the ship to America. He convinced the Queen that these Mennonites would make good patriots for the Queen in British America. She apparently agreed and in order to clear the docks, she supplied the funds for the journey. In addition to the names listed above, there were other families on the ship in 1717.

Lancaster, PA

The following is a list of the family names that settled in and around the Knussli family property which was located about 1 mile west of Lancaster on the Harrisburg Pike that runs through the center of Antonius's property. These names can be seen on the map that follows. Some of the names are interesting names of families that found some fame in America. The last names are Coffman, Musselman, Jacobs, Shelley, Shallenberger, Hershey, Kauffman (4 different properties), and Miller. There was also the Swarr family, located on a nearby property, with a stream named Swarr Run that ran through Antonius's property. The unrelated Nusli family was also located nearby.

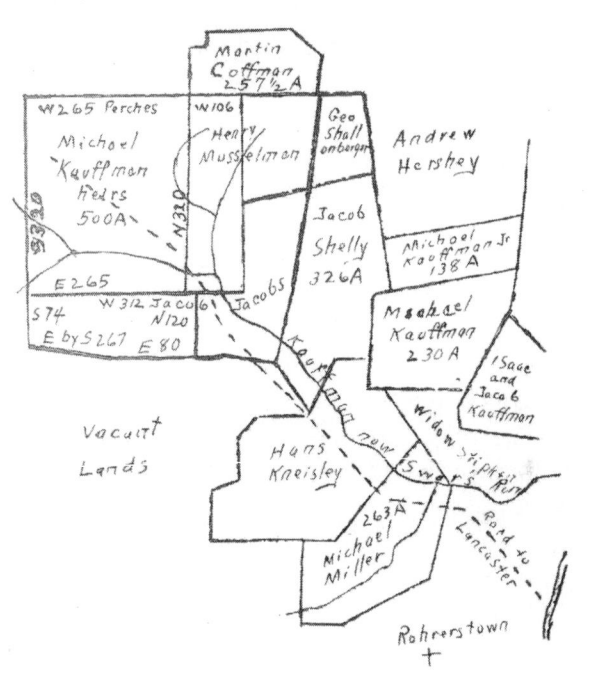

Also on the ship were the Stauffer, Huber, and Brubaker families. It was interesting to discover that descendants of these families were also living or working in and around Ligonier. Mennonite Levi Stauffer is working on the Anthony Nicely Sr. 1810 home near Ligonier and growing up I had a good friend George Stouffer and his family were close neighbors of my family and also part of the Stauffer line. Jim Koontz a descendant of the Brubaker family worked with me at Kennametal and at Compass Inn and Brian Huber a dentist in Ligonier and a member of my church, all had family on the ship that came to Philadelphia in 1717. It was an amazing feeling to discover this coincident.

The Swarr Family History also helped me to determine why the property on the map was shown belonging to Hans Kneisley instead of Antonius. The grant was issued to Antonius Kristopher Knussli in 1717. However, our research never showed him as owning the property. There was discussion among early family researchers that we did not arrive in Lancaster until 1732. This was all explained in the Swarr family history. William Penn died in 1718 before the grants could be finalized and the settlement of his estate took until May of 1732 before it was finalized. This held up not only the processing of the Knussli grant but almost all of the settlers who arrived in 1717. It was in 1727 and 1728 that the naturalization process began to take place. In April 1728, 200 Mennonites signed the documents qualifying them for naturalization. Then the process was stalled because of a new court being established in Lancaster. Finally, on February 14, 1730 the petition was passed allowing them to hold land. However, Penn's estate was not settled until 1732 and the grants could then be finally made. Antonius died on May 14, 1733, with the grant finally issued in 1734, it was issued in the name of his oldest son, Johannes Hans Kneisley, Sr.

The Swarr family history also gave me some additional information on Antonius and Hans. When the property went up for sale after Hans died, the Swaar family bought a section of the property that included the Grinding Mill that was located on the Swarr Run. This was the grinding mill that Antonius and Hans had built and operated. As I said before the Swarr Run ran through the property, and Antonius and Hans took advantage of that and established a Grinding Mill to mill grains into flour. When the land was finally settled many of the children had already moved to other areas and settled.

There was one more event in Antonius's life when he was 73 years of age. He fathered a child by the name of Adam Kneisle to a young woman of about 17 years of age by the name of Elizabeth Yeager. It was noted in his death records that his wife at death was Magdalena Hempstead Knussli and she was listed in his will, however a census of Hempfield Township in 1732 has Antonius listed as having one child in his household listing. Since it was unlikely that Magdalena, at age 68, could have delivered a child and since our family history indicates that Elizabeth Yeager was the wife of Anthony Kneisle and the mother of Adam Kneisle, we feel confident this is the correct connection. Y-DNA also has been used to match my Y-DNA to every one of Antonius's Y-DNA male lines and adding to this that the spelling of Adam's last name in the early 1800,s was Kneisle, which matched closely with the Kneisley spelling of the other children of Antonius. With all of this information, we settled on Adam being the son of Antonius. Adam was the author's link to this family line. So the records now show Antonius with 2 wives, Magdalena Hempstead and Elizabeth Yeager. There were 4 males and 7 females born to Magdalena and 1 male born to Elizabeth.

Antonius died on May 14, 1733 at the age of 75 in Conestoga Manor, Hempfield Township, Lancaster in Pennsylvania, having the honor of being the individual who was our first Knussli ancestor in America. I have been to the area where his property was located and it was a great feeling to go there, knowing I was standing in the area where our family established roots in America. The map below shows the property lines on a present day map of the area. Part of the land today is in housing and part is still in farm condition. You can reach this area from 2 directions. If you are heading west from Philadelphia, PA on the National Highway, (Route 30) before you reach Lancaster, look for the Harrisburg Pike exit and continue to travel west. If you are heading east, from Western PA on Route 30 look for the Harrisburg Pike exit and continue heading east. You need to look for the intersection of the Harrisburg Pike and Sylvan Road. At that location you are on

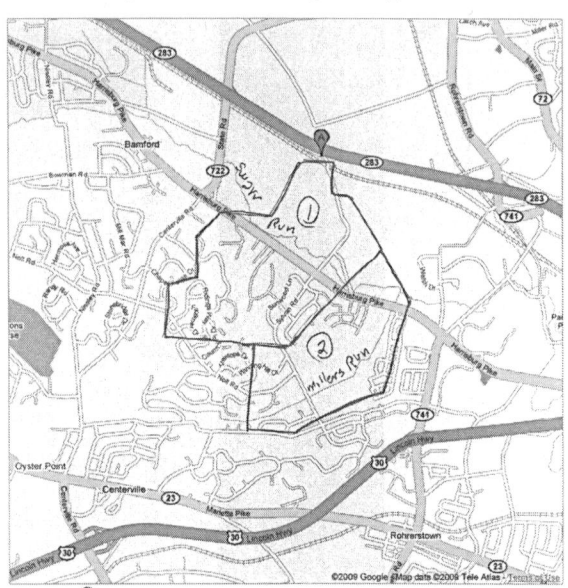

① Hans Kneisley Grant
Antonius Kristopher Knussli, original Property
He was Hans' father.

② Michael Miller Grant

the ¼ eastern section of the original property with a housing development to the south and a farm road leading north with a small bridge just before you reach a barn and farm house. The small bridge is over the Swarr Run and at some point near there would have been Antonius and Han's grinding mill. The mill and original home are no longer standing. At that intersection, if you head west for about a mile Antonius's property would have been on both sides of the Harrisburg Pike. If you have a GPS and locate Sylvan Road in the Lancaster area, it should give you directions to that intersection.

Magdalena Hempstead Knussli died in approximately 1734 at the age of 72. I have not been able to locate a grave site for either her or Antonius. The Mennonite Historical Society in Lancaster has a lot of information on the families who settled this area but after hours of searching along with the help of the library people, I was not able to find any grave information.

It is now time to start telling the story of the different lines of Antonius's family. I am going to go in order of oldest child to youngest child and give you as much family history as I have located on each line. I know I have not covered each of the lines history in an equal manner since some of the lines are lacking the depth of information as the other lines. Perhaps with time more information will come forward on each of the lines. If I have omitted information on a line that you as a family member would like to add please let me know. Perhaps with time either I or someone else will be able to revise the book to expand the history on the lines not covered.

CHAPTER SEVEN

Antonius Kristopher Knussli Sr. Family

Anna Kneisle Kauffman (1678 – 1758)

Anna was the oldest child of Antonius and Magdalena. She was born in 1678 when they were living in the Alsace France area along the Rhine River in Europe. At the age of 18 in 1696, she married Michael Kauffman Sr. in Hassloch, Rheinland, Rheinland-Pfalz, Germany and they were listed in Baldenheim in Alsace in a 1709 Census of the Mennonite areas. She and her husband were listed with the first three of their children and a brother to Michael. Before they left that area, they had five children. The sixth child was not listed in that Census and we are not sure where he was born but we believe he was also born in Alsace before they made the trip to Lancaster along with Anna's father and mother and siblings and the parents, Isaac and Elizabeth Mergerdt Kauffman and siblings of Michael Kauffman. When Michael and Anna arrived in 1717 in Lancaster they had six children, John b. 1700, Catherine Elizabeth b. 1703, Martin (who later became a Minister) b. 1709, Michael Joseph b. June 21, 1714, Christian b. 1715, and David b. ca 1716. Anna's husband Michael died in 1718 after arriving and settling in Lancaster. A few years later, Anna remarried to Jacob Jacobs, who owned property adjoining the Knuslli property. It is not clear, if Anna had possession of the land and when she married Jacob that he took ownership or if this land was granted to Jacob at the time of his arrival in 1717. Most of the land granted in 1717 was never deeded until after 1730, so it could have been Michael Kauffman's original land.

The history records show that Anna died on June 24, 1758 in Hawksbill Settlement in Luray County in VA. Her sister Christina Kniseley Haldiman and her husband, who was a Mennonite Missionary, and their family, had moved to that area many years before. Three of Anna's sons had also moved to VA and one or both of them were also working as Missionaries to the Native Americans living in that area. It appears that since her husband Jacob Jacobs had died before 1757, Anna may have moved to VA to live with one of her sons and near her sister. She died several months prior to the Indian raid that ended with her sister and several other family members being killed. There are two comments on her death. One says she died peacefully in her sleep and another indicates she was also killed in an Indian raid. There were numerous raids from 1755 through 1758, so the possibility exists that she could have been killed in a separate raid from the one where her sister was killed.

I have only a limited history on this branch. Their son John Kauffman married Ann Bomberger and they lived and died in Landisville near Lancaster, PA. Their son Rev. Martin Kauffman married Barbara Stauffer, who had been previously married to Martin Nissley. Martin and his wife Barbara had also moved to VA in Page County and he was working as a Mennonite Missionary.

Their son Michael Kauffman married his cousin Barbara Kneissle Haldiman and after she died, he married Magdalena Stauffer. I do not have any information on the children from either wife. Michael had also moved to VA with his family and lived in Rockingham County.

Son David moved to Shenandoah County in VA and there is no information on his family. There is no information on their daughter Catherine or on their son Christian.

There are 16 Cauffman families and hundreds of Kauffman families listed in the VA online telephone directory and since both spellings were used for this line, many of these listed individuals could be related to Anna.

Following is the limited list of names, I have available on the family line, showing descendants and spouses.

1-Michael KAUFFMAN Sr. (16 March 1674/5-1718)
+Anna KNEISLE (1678-24 June 1758)
    2-John KAUFFMAN (1700-1759)
    +Ann BOMBERGER (about 1701-before 1781)
    2-Catherine Elizabeth KAUFFMAN (1703-before 1783)
    2-Rev. Martin KAUFFMAN (1709-1749)
    +Barbara STAUFFER (about 1725-before 1804)
    2-Michael Joseph KAUFFMAN (21 June 1714-21 December 1788)

+Barbara Kneissle HALDIMAN (1718-24 February 1764)
+Magdalena STAUFFER (1720-7 March 1787)
2-Christian KAUFFMAN (1715-before 1795)
2-David KAUFFMAN (circa 1716-before 1806)

Christina Kneisle Haldiman (1684 – 1758)

Christina was the second oldest child of Antonius and Magdalena. She was born in Muttersholtz Alsace in 1684 and was listed in the 1709 Census living in Jebsheim Germany with her husband Christian Haldiman. Christian's parents were Michael and Madlena Gerber Haldiman. He was born on May 13, 1677 in Sorbach, Eggiwill, in the Canton of Berne in Switzerland. Christina and Christian also made the move to Lancaster at the same time as Christina's father and family. Christian and Christina had 2 children that came with them to America in 1717, Jacob, born in 1715 and John, born in 1716, both were born in Muttersholtz, Alsace, France. Their 3rd child, Barbara was born in 1718 in Augusta Co., VA, which indicates they did not stay long in Lancaster, PA before they moved to into VA. History on that area indicates there was a group of Mennonites settlers moved there in 1726 or 1727, so it appears they were already there when the new group moved there.

Their Ministry in VA was to convert the Native Americans to Christianity and for quite a number of years, they moved among the different tribes without difficulty. In the summer of 1758, there was the beginning of pressures to have the Native Americans leave that area. The French and Indian War started to develop in 1754 and this was causing strife between the Native Americans and the British settlers who were expanding into the Native American lands. In 1755 through 1758, there were numerous raids and attacks on the settlers by the Pontiac and Shawnee tribes. These attacks were being spurred by the French and many settlers were captured or lost their lives. In August of 1758, Christina was living with her son Jacob and his wife Maria at their home with Jacob's children, while her husband Christian and her son Jacob were out of the area on Missionary duties. The attack was swift and vicious. Jacob's wife

Maria attempted to protect her children and fought the Indians, They tomahawked her and killed her and killed her mother Christina. Then they killed the two young daughters' and the baby by bashing its head against a tree. The 2 or 3 young sons put up a fight and it amused the Indians so they took them as prisoners. One died shortly after leaving the area and one or two were released after the treaty of 1762. It is reported a Christian Haldiman survived and returned. Christina's son Jacob stayed in VA and I do not have any further information other than it is reported he died in the Hawksbill Settlement.

There are only a few Haldiman families listed in the VA online phone directory. Following is a complete list of all the descendants and spouses that I have available for this family line:

1-Christian HALDIMAN (13 May 1677-circa 1764)
+Christina KNEISLEY (1684-August 1758)
    2-Jacob Kneisle HALDIMAN (1715-before 1805)
    +Maria Catarina BOIN (about 1716-August 1758)
        3-Christoper HALDIMAN (1741-1810)
        +Eve UNKNOWN (about 1742-before 1822)
            4-George HALDIMAN (1772-before 1830)
            4-Cfristian HALDIMAN (about 1780-before 1870)
            4-Eve or Eva HALDIMAN (1799-13 March 1837)
            +Eligan Reynolds EVANS (about 1798-before 1836)
    2-John Kneisle HALDIMAN (1716-before 1806)
    2-Barbara Kneisle HALDIMAN (1718-24 February 1764)
    +Michael Joseph KAUFFMAN (21 June 1714-21 December 1788)

Johannes Hans Kneisley Sr. (1688 – 1757)

Johannes, was the 3rd child and oldest son of Antonius and Magdalena, and was born in the Alsace Providence on the French side of the Rhine River in 1688 and died on June 15, 1757 in Hempfield Twp. Lancaster Co., PA. His name followed the general practice of the time by the first son being named after his paternal grandfather. He was listed in the 1707 Census in Alsace as being 19 years old and still living with his parents. He married Mary Christina Sechrist circa 1715 in Alsace. She was the daughter of

Michael and Anna Sechrist and was born circa 1700 and died after 1757. He was named as the owner of Antonius's property as I explained in the previous chapter. As was the practice in those days, the oldest son inherited most of the property of the father. Hans and Mary had 11 children. The first listed was born in 1719 which was after they moved to America. It is not known if they had children before they left Alsace who may have died due to the rigors of the travel to America. The list of their children is shown below as the 2nd generation in the descendant list. The 3rd generations listed below are the grandchildren.

There is a tremendous amount of history on this family line. It takes 233 pages to print a full narrative register report with all the notes on all of their descendants. There are 562 different family Surnames in the descendant list and there are 9 different spellings of the Knusli name. It takes 22 pages to print out a list of all the descendants of Hans and his wife. This line has moved to many different locations and has spread to at least 27 of the US States and Canada.

Following is a 3 generations list of the descendants and spouses of this family line:

```
     1-Johannes Hans KNEISLEY Sr. (1688-15 June 1757)
+Mary Christina SECHRIST (circa 1700-after 1757)
    2-John Hans KNEISLY Jr. (1719-28 May 1787)
    +Mary SHONAUER (1719-1760)
        3-John KNEISLY III (29 February 1748-November 1819)
        3-Michael KNEISLY (29 March 1751-2 August 1793)
        3-Barbara KNEISLY (11 November 1752-before 1842)
        3-Abraham KNEISLY (1754-before 1756)
        3-Christian KNEISLY (1757-5 September 1836)
        3-Abraham KNEISLY (21 March 1759-before 1760)
        3-Mary Magdalena KNEISLY (18 October 1760-October 1820)
    +Elizabeth BYER (about 1731-circa 1783)
        3-Elizabeth KNEISLY (21 October 1762-before 1852)
        3-Henry KNEISLY (6 March 1766-before 1856)
    +Christiana UNKNOWN (about 1764-before 1854)
        3-Marrei "Mary" KNEISLY (25 February 1785-before 1875)
        3-Daniel KNEISLY (18 March 1786-26 January 1880)
        3-David KNISLEY (12 March 1787-28 December 1860)
```

2-Beverly (Barbara?) KNEISLEY (1722-before 1802)
+John HARNISH (about 1721-before 1801)
2-Anna KNEISLEY (1724-before 1809)
+Jacob FULWILER/FOLWELL (about 1723-before 1775)
    3-John FULWILER (circa 1745-before 1835)
    3-Michael FULWILER (circa 1747-before 1837)
    3-Jacob FULWILER (circa 1743-before 1833)
    3-Magdalena FULWILER (circa 1751-before 1841)
    3-Mary FULWILER (circa 1753-before 1843)
2-Mary Magdelena KNEISLEY (1725-after 1775)
+John MUMMA (about 1724-before 1804)
2-Anthony KNEISLY Sr. (7 March 1728-23 November 1801)
+Mary Ann DAUGHERTY (6 May 1730-25 October 1789)
    3-Anna Belle KNEISLY (16 August 1750-23 June 1824)
    3-John Samuel KNISELY Sr. (21 Sep. 1752-23 Sep. 1853)
    3-Anthony K. KNEISLY Jr. (14 August 1754-14 Nov. 1818)
    3-Eva May KNEISLY (20 May 1756-12 September 1831)
    3-Abraham KNEISLY (15 September 1759-13 May 1842)
    3-Michael KNEISLY (25 January 1761-12 December 1822)
    3-Jacob KNEISLY (22 March 1764-17 May 1843)
    3-Mary KNEISLY (2 February 1766-16 September 1848)
    3-Samuel KNEISLY Sr. (6 February 1768-7 January 1844)
    3-George Washington KNEISLY Sr. (10 Apr. 1770-before 1860)
2-Abraham KNEISLEY (1727-1764)
+Mary HOW (about 1728-before 1808)
    3-George KNEISLEY (circa 1749-before 1839)
    3-Solomon KNEISLEY (circa 1751-before 1841)
    3-Samuel KNEISLEY (circa 1753-before 1843)
    3-John KNEISLEY (circa 1755-before 1845)
    3-Barbara KNEISLEY (circa 1757-before 1847)
2-Michael KNEISLEY (2 February 1727-3 August 1793)
+Barbara Anna BAER (29 August 1734-29 June 1793)
    3-Mary KNEISLY (circa 1753-before 1843)
    3-Abraham KNEISLY (circa 1755-before 1845)
    3-Malli KNEISLY (circa 1757-before 1847)
    3-Rebecca KNEISLY (circa 1759-before 1849)
    3-Elizabeth KNEISLY (circa 1761-before 1851)
    3-John KNEISLY (circa 1763-before 1853)
    3-Anna KNEISLY (circa 1765-before 1855)
    3-Barbara KNEISLY (circa 1767-before 1857)
    3-Susanna KNEISLY (circa 1769-before 1795)

2-Maria "Mary" KNEISLEY (1731-before 1811)
+Conrad BEAVER (BIEBER) (about 1730-before 1810)
2-Joseph KNEISLEY (1736-before 1773)
2-Peter KNEISLEY (1737-before 1817)
2-Christian KNEISLY (23 April 1757-1836)
+Anna STEINER (about 1761-before 1851)
    3-Feria KNEISLY (20 November 1783-1815)
    3-Elizabeth KNISLEY (26 June 1784-1827)
    3-Mali KNISLEY (3 October 1787-1802)
    3-Anna KNISLEY (15 August 1790-8 February 1863)
    3-Rachael KNISLEY (11 September 1793-1847)
    3-John K KNISLEY (8 March 1796-1870)
    3-Samuel KNISLEY (16 May 1799-25 January 1873)
    3-Christian KNEISLY (18 July 1802-1846)
    3-Jacob KNISLEY (22 April 1805-5 November 1867)
    3-Maria KNISLEY (4 April 1807-1863)

There are certain members of this line that I will cover in a later chapter. I will do this for each line to highlight people of note or stories of interest. The following people, Christian Kneisly, George Omit Deise, Thomas Alexander Deise, Melvin Henry Knisely, Jacob (Jake) Clarence Knisely, Robert August Knisely, Rev. Harry Lee Knisely, Michael Douglas Nicely Sr., Alexander (Alex) Knisely, and Dr. Jonathan P. Knisely, are people of note or with interesting stories that are members of this line.

Antonius Kristopher (Anthony) Kneussel Jr. (1693 – 1778)

Antonius Jr. was the 4th child and 2nd son of Antonius and Magdalena and he was born in Alsace in 1693 and died on August 28, 1778 in Woodstock, Shenandoah County, VA. His name also followed normal procedure by the 2nd son being named the same as his father. He was listed in the 1707 census in Alsace and listed as age 14 and still living with his parents. He married Anna Barbara Doerr on July 22, 1734 in Lancaster County in PA. She was the daughter of John and Mary (unknown last name) Doerr and was born in 1715 in the Canton of Bern in Switzerland and died before 1778 in Woodstock, Shenandoah Co., VA. It is likely her father, mother, and family moved to America in 1717 along with the other

Mennonite families who came at that time. There is no exact information when Antonius and Anna moved to VA but they were married in 1734 in Lancaster and their 1st child was born in 1737 in Warrington Co., VA, so they apparently moved to VA between 1734 and 1737. Antonius and Anna had 10 children. The list of their children is shown below as the 2nd generation in the descendant list. The 3rd generations listed below are the grandchildren.

There is a tremendous amount of history on this family line. It takes 147 pages to print a full narrative register report with all the notes on all of their descendants. There are 309 different family Surnames in the descendant list and there are 6 different spellings of the Knusli name. It takes 44 pages to print out a list of all the descendants of Hans and his wife. This line has moved to many different locations and has spread to at least 23 of the US States and Canada.

Following is a 3 generations list of the descendants and spouses of this family line:

1-Antonius Kristopher "Anthony" KNEUSSEL Jr. (1695-28 Aug. 1778)
+Anna Barbara DOERR (1715-before 1778)
    2-Elizabeth Barbara KNICELEY (15 February 1736-1804)
    +Ulrich MILLER (circa 1735-before 1825)
    2-John George KNICELEY (18 December 1737-9 July 1804)
    +Mary Magdalen KRAUSE (about 1738-before 1818)
        3-Jacob "Jack" NICELY Sr. (1756-1836)
        3-Catherine KNEISLY (about 1758-before 1838)
        3-John M. KNEISLY Sr. (1760-21 April 1845)
        3-Elizabeth KNEISLY (about 1762-before 1842)
        3-Mardeline KNEISLY (about 1764-before 1844)
        3-Margaretha KNEISLY (about 1766-before 1846)
        3-George KNISELY (1768-20 February 1820)
        3-Simon NEISLE (about 1770-before 1850)
        3-Susan Maria NEISLE (about 1774-before 1854)
        3-Henry NICELY (1780-before 1870)
        3-David KNEISLY (1792-1855)
    2-Christina Susanna KNISELY (23 April 1739-before 1819)
    2-Anthony A. KNICELEY III (10 December 1740-19 March 1799)
    +Anna Barbara MOURER (1750-1805)
        3-Mary KNICELEY (1769-28 October 1855)
        3-Elizabeth KNICELEY (10 February 1773-before 1863)

3-John Henry KNICELEY (21 October 1773-before 1863)
3-Anthony A. KNICELEY IV (1775-1861)
3-Barbara KNICELEY (1776-1847)
3-Rebecca KNICELEY (about 1780-before 1870)
3-Jacob Squires KNICELEY (1781-1836)
3-Christine KNICELEY (1 November 1781-before 1861)
3-David KNICELEY (1782-before 1873)
3-Racheal KNICELEY (11 July 1790-20 November 1847)
2-Jacob KNISELEY Sr. (26 March 1741-1 March 1830)
+Elizabeth Susannah NYE (1750-circa 1825)
    3-Rhuben (or Reuben) KNISELEY (1766-before 1856)
    3-Chapman J. KNISELEY (circa 1767-before 1857)
    3-John David KNEISLEY (22 November 1768-14 October 1860)
    3-Rebecca Jane KNISELEY (1764-1776)
    3-Henry KNISELEY (1780-before 1870)
    3-Mary "Polly" KNISELEY (circa 1781-10 April 1833)
    3-Barbara KNISELEY (circa 1788-before 1878)
    3-Jacob M. KNISELEY Jr. (circa 1789-before 1879)
    3-Samuel KNISELEY (circa 1794-before 1884)
    3-Elizabeth KNISELEY (9 June 1795-December 1862)
    3-Susanna (or Hannah) KNISELEY (20 Nov. 1799-before 1889)
    3-Adam KNISELEY (1 March 1801-before 1891)
2-Michael KNICELEY (about 1742-1831)
+Catherine UNKNOWN (about 1743-before 1823)
    3-Jonas "John" KNICELEY Sr. (1769-20 May 1817)
    3-John NICELY (circa 1772-before 1860)
2-Catherine Elizabeth KNISELY (4 February 1744-before 1824)
+Jacob FULWILER (circa 1743-before 1833)
    3-John FULWILER (circa 1765-before 1855)
2-Anna Regina KNICELEY (4 April 1745-before 1825)
2-Samuel (or Simon) KNICELEY Sr. (7 July 1745-before 1835)
+Mary WOLF (circa 1739-1837)
    3-Catherine KNICELEY (circa 1760-circa 1845)
    3-Samuel KNICELEY Jr. (circa 1766-before 1856)
    3-Michael KNICELEY (circa 1774-before 1864)
    3-Jacob KNICELEY (circa 1776-)
    3-Anthony KNICELEY (circa 1778-before 1868)
2-Mary Magdalena KNISELY (about 1747-before 1827)
+Jacob SHELBY (about 1746-before 1826)

There are certain members of this line that I will cover in a later chapter. I will do this for each line to highlight people of note or stories of interest. The following people, Jonas "John" Kniseley, Gillion "Gil" Niceley, James "Jim" Bernard Niceley, Sen. Frank Samuel Niceley and Dwaine Larry Nicely are people of note or with interesting stories that are members of this line.

Elizabeth Kneisly Kauffman (1696 – 1761)

Elizabeth was the 5th child and 3rd daughter of Antonius and Magdalena and was born in the Alsace Providence on the French side of the Rhine River in 1696 and died in 1761 most likely in the Lancaster, PA area. She was listed in the 1707 Census in Alsace as 11 years old and still living with her parents. She married Andreas Kauffman in 1725. They had one son Andrew Coffman II. I do not have a record of any other children, but more research may turn up others. Note that Andrew changed the spelling of his name and all of his descendants went by Coffman. Andreas died in 1743 and Elizabeth remarried to Christian Stoneman in ca 1744. There were no children of this marriage. Later descendants of Andreas and Elizabeth moved to Tennessee and then later generations to Missouri. A check of the phone directory shows that the name Coffman is located in most of the 50 states. I am not sure if all are related. Again, I have not spent any time on researching this line and I have not been contacted by any Coffman descendants.

Following is a complete list of all the descendants and spouses that I have available for this family line:

1-Elizabeth KNEISLEY (1698-1761)
+Andreas KAUFFMAN (about 1690-1743)
    2-Andrew COFFMAN II (1729-1763)
    +Magdaline MARTIN (1731-1758)
        3-Christian COFFMAN (circa 1751-before 1841)
        3-Elizabeth COFFMAN (circa 1752-before 1842)
        3-Jacob COFFMAN (circa 1753-before 1843)
        3-Magdalena COFFMAN (circa 1754-before 1844)
        3-David COFFMAN (circa 1755-before 1845)
        3-Fraena COFFMAN (circa 1756-before 1846)

        3-Infant COFFMAN (circa 1757-circa 1757)
        3-Andrew COFFMAN III (17 October 1760-May 1846)
        +Unknown UNKNOWN (circa 1761-before 1813)
            4-David COFFMAN (19 January 1787-11 July 1838)
            +Mary Susanah BUNCH (1796-before 1863)
                5-Mary Ann Elizabeth COFFMAN (ca 1814-before 1904)
                5-Anna COFFMAN (circa 1815-before 1905)
            4-Nancy Polly COFFMAN (6 May 1791-1844)
+Christian STONEMAN (circa 1697-before 1787)

Maria Knussli (about 1700 – bef. 1717)

Maria, was the 6th child and 4th daughter of Antonius and Magdalena, and was born in the Alsace Providence on the French side of the Rhine River in 1700 and was listed in the 1707 census as age 7 and living with her parents. We are unsure of her death. She was never listed in any of the paperwork or wills of the family in Lancaster, so she may have died before the family left for America in 1717 or there is also the possibility she may have married and she and her husband decided to stay in Europe.

Jacob Knussli (about 1701 – bef. 1706)

Jacob, was the 7th child and 3rd son of Antonius and Magdalena, and was born in the Alsace Providence on the French side of the Rhine River about 1701 and died in Alsace before the 1707 census. If his name followed standard procedure, he would have been named after Magdalena's father. Since we do not know Magdalena's father's name it is most likely Jacob Hempstead.

Barbara Kneisley Miller (1703 – 1777)

Barbara, was the 8th child and 5th daughter of Antonius and Magdalena, and was born in the Alsace Providence on the French side of the Rhine River in 1703 and was listed in the 1707 census in Alsace as age 4 and living with her parents. She married Michael Miller in 1726 in the Lancaster area and their property was a 263 acre farm east and south of Antonius's original property. Michael was born in 1690 in Zurich Switzerland and died on August 20, 1739 in Lancaster and it is apparent he was on the same journey to America as the Knussli family in 1717 due to the location of his property. It is not known if he was married before he married Barbara, but he was 27 years old when they married. Barbara and Michael had seven children between 1726 and 1739. You will see them listed as the 2nd generation on the listing below. After Michael passed away, Barbara married Frederick L. Woolslegel in 1745. There were no children from this marriage.

There is a crossover in this line. Mary "Elizabeth" Miller, daughter of David Miller and Grand Daughter of Michael and Barbara Kneisley Miller married a John Knisely who is a descendant of the second branch of our family that moved from Eggiwil, Canton of Bern in Switzerland to America in 1739. As I mentioned earlier, I will cover more on this line in a later section. As far as I can find this is the only link between the 2 lines in America. They would have been around 3rd to 4th cousins, depending on where the link occurred in Switzerland. Perhaps someday we will find the exact link in Switzerland.

Other than Mary's family line, this is also a short line with at least one of their children, Samuel Miller moving to Harrisonburg, Rockingham, VA.

Except for Mary's line, the following is a complete list of all the descendants and spouses available for this family line:

1-Michael MILLER (1690-20 August 1739)
+Barbara KNEISLEY (1706-1777)
....2-Michael MILLER Jr. (about 1727-1771)
....+Susanna UNKNOWN (about 1728-before 1803)
....2-David MILLER (about 1728-before 1813)
....+Unknown UNKNOWN (about 1734-before 1824)
........3-Mary "Elizabeth?" MILLER (21 September 1757-before 1847)
........+John KNISELY Sr. (21 September 1752-21 December 1834)
............4-George KNEISLY (about 1777-1819)
............4-Abraham KNISELY (16 February 1778-28 December 1841)
............4-Salome Sarah KNISELY (16 Nov. 1780-16 Nov. 1820)
............4-John KNISELY Jr. (27 August 1782-before 1830)
............4-Samuel A. KNISELEY (November 1784-2 June 1867)

............4-Elizabeth KNISELY (11 November 1787-11 March 1867)
............4-Jacob KNISELY (15 February 1789-15 February 1833)
............4-David Peter KNISELY (8 July 1792-4 September 1877)
............4-Joseph KNISELY (1795-17 April 1882)
............4-Mary KNISELY (19 February 1796-3 February 1874)
............4-Susan KNISELY (1797-before 1887)
....2-Elizabeth MILLER (about 1729-1794)
....+Abraham WOLGEMUTH (about 1734-before 1814)
....2-Samuel MILLER (1730-17 February 1788)
....+Magdalena WILEY (about 1738-17 February 1788)
....2-Christian E. MILLER (1732-before 1803)
....+Catherine HAGIN (about 1724-before 1804)
....2-Barbara MILLER (about 1737-before 1817)
....+Samuel WOLGEMUTH (about 1736-before 1826)
....2-Maudlin MILLER (about 1739-before 1819)
....+Peter BOSSLER (about 1738-before 1818)

Sybilla Kneisley Golladay (1707 – 1758)

Sybilla, was the 9th child and 6th daughter of Antonius and Magdalena, and was born in the Alsace Providence on the French side of the Rhine River in 1707 and was listed in the 1707 census in Alsace as new born and living with her parents. She married Joseph Golladay in 1733 in the Lancaster area. I do not have any further information on where their property was located and whether Joseph's family had moved into the area in 1717 with the other Mennonite families. Their property was a 263 acre farm east and south of Antonius's original property. I do not have any birth or death information on Joseph and no information on his parents. Sybilla and Joseph had 2 children and you can see them listed as the 2nd generation on the listing below.

1-Joseph GOLLADAY (about 1708-before 1788)
+Sybilla KNEISLEY (KNUSLI) (1709-21 May 1758)
....2-Joseph GOLLADAY (circa 1733-23 May 1758)
....2-Jacob GOLLADAY Sr. (1735-28 February 1795)

Mary Kneisley Shelley Landis (1708 – 1758)

Mary was the 10th child and the 7th daughter of Antonius and Magdalena. Since she was born after the census of 1707 but still born before the family left Alsace so she was also born in the Alsace Providence on the french side of the Rhine River 1708. Her year of birth was based on family information. She married Jacob Shelly Sr. circa 1727 in the Lancaster area. He was born circa 1690 and died in 1752 in the Lancaster area. There is no firm information as to when he or his family came to America. Mary and Jacob had 9 children, 7 males and 2 females. After Jacob died, Mary married Henry Landis. Two descendants of the Landis line started a company named Landis Machine in 1889 and still it exists today as a supplier of machine tools used in manufacturing of durable products. Mary and Henry did not have any children. I have information on 2 of Mary and Jacob's male lines but none on the female lines. There are several interesting things about the Shelley name. There is a Shelley Island in the Susquehanna River south of Harrisburg. Some of the Shelley members lived on this island and many of the descendants are buried in a cemetery located on the island.

There is also a Shelly Lake and recreation area in Raleigh, NC that was near where I lived during my 17 years in Raleigh. I have not been able to find information on how it received the name but there are still 19 Shelley families living in Raleigh. I suspect that a descendant of Jacob and Mary ended up living there and perhaps donated the land to the city for the park.

The following list covers 5 generations of this family and is all the information I have available. Since this line is not as long as several of the other family lines are, I am listing all the descendants I have in my file.

1-Jacob SHELLEY Sr. (about 1690-1752)
+Mary KNEISLEY (KNUSLI) (circa 1708-24 June 1758)
....2-Jacob SHELLEY Jr. (circa 1728-1790)
....+Anna PEELMAN (BEIDELMAN) (circa 1729-before 1819)
........3-Jacob SHELLEY III (1765-1839)
........+Maria Margaretta SCHWEITZER (ca 1766-bef. 1856)
........3-Barbara Catherine E. SHELLEY (circa 1766-before 1856)

........3-Mary SHELLEY (1767-1849)
........+John KROUSE (circa 1765-1840)
....2-Abraham SHELLEY (circa 1730-before 1820)
....2-Anna SHELLEY (circa 1732-before 1822)
....2-Christian SHELLEY (circa 1734-before 1824)
....2-Daniel SHELLEY Sr. (1735-21 June 1802)
....+Elizabeth LANE (1735-1766)
........3-Jacob SHELLEY (1760-1801)
........+Anna RIEFF (circa 1761-circa 1792)
............4-Isaac SHELLEY (circa 1781-before 1871)
............4-Elizabeth SHELLEY (circa 1783-before 1873)
............4-Daniel SHELLEY (circa 1785-before 1875)
............4-Nancy SHELLEY (circa 1787-before 1877)
............4-Polly SHELLEY (circa 1789-before 1879)
............4-Anna SHELLEY (circa 1791-before 1881)
........+Mary UNKNOWN (circa 1765-before 1875)
........3-Michael SHELLEY (1762-before 1852)
........3-Susanah SHELLEY (1763-before 1853)
........3-Abraham SHELLEY (1764-1815)
........+Anna UNKNOWN (circa 1765-circa 1792)
............4-Catharina SHELLEY (1790-2 December 1831)
............+Martin CRULL (circa 1789-before 1879)
................5-Elizabeth CRULL (27 Feb. 1807-Sep. 1880)
................5-Abraham CRULL (27 Nov. 1809-before 1899)
................5-Jacob Morris CRULL (circa 1812-before 1902)
................5-Susanna CRULL (Feb. 1820-Sep. 1838)
........+Maria SHUMAN (circa 1767-before 1801)
............4-Catherine SHELLEY (circa 1794-before 1884)
............4-Elizabeth SHELLEY (circa 1796-before 1886)
............4-Anna SHELLEY (circa 1798-before 1888)
............4-Molly "Polly" SHELLEY (circa 1800-before 1890)
........+Rebecca DETWILER (circa 1775-before 1865)
........3-Daniel SHELLEY Jr. (1766-1825)
........+Elizabeth SHUMAN (1770-1827)
............4-Margaret SHELLEY (1788-1811)
............4-John SHELLEY (1790-1852)
............+Catherine DONALDSON (circa 1791-before 1881)
................5-Elizabeth SHELLEY (1817-before 1907)

................+Unknown BEAR (circa 1816-before 1906)
................5-Daniel SHELLEY (1819-1820)
................5-Rosanna SHELLEY (1821-1825)
................5-John SHELLEY (circa 1822-before 1912)
................5-Samuel SHELLEY (1824-1885)
................+Christina FINK (1829-1892)
................5-Christian SHELLEY (1837-1843)
............4-Daniel SHELLEY III (1791-before 1881)
............+Catherine ETTER (circa 1792-before 1882)
................5-bsolom SHELLEY (circa 1810-before 1900)
................5-Anne E. SHELLEY (circa 1812-before 1902)
................5-Mary L. SHELLEY (circa 1814-before 1904)
................5-Henry E. SHELLEY (circa 1816-before 1906)
................5-Susan SHELLEY (circa 1818-before 1908)
................5-Franklin SHELLEY (circa 1820-before 1910)
............4-Catherine SHELLEY (1793-before 1883)
............4-Abraham SHELLEY (1795-1795)
............4-Elizabeth SHELLEY (1797-before 1887)
............+John SHAEFER (circa 1798-before 1888)
................5-Bartram SHAEFER (circa 1816-before 1906)
................5-Ella SHAEFER (circa 1818-before 1908)
................5-Susan SHAEFER (circa 1820-before 1910)
............4-Jacob SHELLEY (1798-before 1888)
............+Elizabeth ALLEN (1820-19 August 1849)
................5-Christian SHELLEY (circa 1839-before 1929)
................5-Nancy SHELLEY (circa 1841-before 1931)
................5-Mary SHELLEY (circa 1843-before 1933)
............4-Wendel SHELLEY (1801-28 January 1873)
............+Mary Elizabeth FLORY (1 Aug. 1804-Nov. 1889)
................5-Daniel SHELLEY (4 June 1819-8 August 1820)
................5-Leah SHELLEY (circa 1825-before 1915)
................5-John SHELLEY (27 October 1839-before 1929)
............4-Christian SHELLEY (1804-1894)
............+Catherine WOLFE (circa 1805-1838)
............+Elizabeth Ann DORMAN (circa 1807-before 1887)
................5-Lyndia SHELLEY (circa 1840-before 1930)
................5-Adiline SHELLEY (circa 1842-before 1932)
................5-Oliver SHELLEY (circa 1844-before 1934)

............5-Christian SHELLEY (circa 1846-before 1936)
............5-Henriatte SHELLEY (circa 1848-before 1938)
............5-Catherine SHELLEY (circa 1850-before 1940)
..........4-Susannah SHELLEY (1804-1805)
..........4-Abraham SHELLEY (1809-1895)
..........+Annie HESS (circa 1810-circa 1843)
............5-Edward SHELLEY (circa 1828-before 1918)
............5-Mary SHELLEY (circa 1830-before 1920)
............5-Clymer SHELLEY (circa 1832-before 1922)
............5-Lewis SHELLEY (circa 1834-before 1924)
............5-Latimar SHELLEY (circa 1836-before 1926)
............5-Swiler SHELLEY (circa 1838-before 1928)
............5-Mina SHELLEY (circa 1840-before 1930)
............5-Elizabeth SHELLEY (circa 1842-before 1932)
..........+Harietta CRULL (circa 1820-before 1910)
............5-Bartram SHELLEY (circa 1845-before 1935)
............5-Henry SHELLEY (1847-before 1937)
............5-Walter SHELLEY (circa 1849-before 1939)
............5-Abraham SHELLEY (circa 1851-before 1941)
............5-Martin SHELLEY (circa 1853-before 1943)
............5-Oliver SHELLEY (circa 1855-before 1945)
............5-Danie SHELLEY (circa 1857-before 1947)
............5-Jane SHELLEY (circa 1859-before 1949)
............5-Mary E. SHELLEY (circa 1861-before 1951)
..........4-Isaac SHELLEY (1811-1811)
..........4-Lydia SHELLEY (1813-1908)
..........+John CRULL (1818-1876)
............5-Martin CRULL (circa 1837-before 1927)
............5-Abraham CRULL (circa 1839-before 1929)
............5-Elmira J. CRULL (circa 1841-before 1931)
............5-Arabella CRULL (circa 1843-before 1933)
....+Catherine GRAFF (circa 1750-before 1777)
........3-Catherine SHELLEY (1772-1849)
........+Joseph RIFE (circa 1771-before 1861)
..........4-Joseph RIFE (circa 1791-before 1881)
..........4-Joseph RIFE (circa 1793-before 1883)
........3-Johannes SHELLEY (1775-April 1828)
........+Lydia HERMAN (9 August 1775-circa 1795)

........+Lydia SHUMAN (circa 1778-before 1868)
..........4-John Moses SHELLEY (1799-1835)
..........4-Daniel SHELLEY (6 December 1800-1802)
..........4-Benjiman Franklin SHELLEY (18 Jan. 1806-7 Mar. 1807)
..........4-Herman SHELLEY (13 Sep. 1807-23 Dec. 1845)
....+Elizabeth GRAFF (circa 1752-before 1781)
........3-Elizabeth SHELLEY (1777-1828)
........+Jacob BEAR (circa 1776-before 1866)
........3-Mary Ann SHELLEY (1780-1841)
........+Henry ETTER (circa 1779-before 1869)
..........4-Anna ETTER (circa 1799-before 1889)
..........4-Polly ETTER (circa 1801-before 1891)
....+Barbara NISSLEY (NUSLI) (1754-before 1834)
........3-Wendel SHELLEY (1781-1831)
........+Anna RIFE (29 April 1773-22 March 1815)
..........4-David SHELLEY (circa 1806-before 1896)
..........4-Susan SHELLEY (circa 1808-before 1898)
..........4-Michael SHELLEY (2 January 1809-3 January 1865)
..........+Elizabeth Elmira CRULL (6 Feb. 1814-before 1904)
............5-Ephrium SHELLEY (10 July 1833-1836)
..........4-Elizabeth SHELLEY (circa 1811-before 1901)
..........4-Lydia SHELLEY (circa 1813-before 1903)
..........4-Leah SHELLEY (circa 1815-before 1905)
........3-Michael SHELLEY (1782-before 1872)
........3-Susannah SHELLEY (1783-1824)
........+Henry RIFE (circa 1782-before 1872)
..........4-Jacob RIFE (circa 1802-before 1892)
..........4-Daniel RIFE (circa 1804-before 1894)
..........4-Mary RIFE (circa 1806-before 1896)
..........4-Abraham RIFE (circa 1808-before 1898)
..........4-John RIFE (circa 1810-before 1900)
........3-Mary SHELLEY (1784-before 1874)
........+John LONGNECKER (circa 1783-before 1873)
........3-Rachel SHELLEY (1787-before 1877)
........+Melchior BRENNEMAN (circa 1786-before 1816)
........+William REIDER (circa 1786-before 1876)
..........4-Rachel REIDER (circa 1816-before 1906)

............4-Henry REIDER (circa 1818-before 1908)
............4-Leah REIDER (circa 1820-before 1910)
........3-Mary Polly SHELLEY (1790-before 1880)
........+Henry SHEAR (circa 1789-before 1879)
....2-Martin SHELLEY (circa 1737-before 1827)
....2-Mary SHELLEY (circa 1739-before 1829)
....2-Michael SHELLEY (circa 1741-before 1831)
....2-Peter SHELLEY (circa 1743-before 1833)

George H. Kneisley (1711 – 1785)

George was the 11th child and 4th son of Antonius and Magdalena and was born in the Alsace Providence on the French side of the Rhine River on September 4, 1711. There was no Census information after the 1707 census, so the date of birth was obtained from family records in Lancaster. He married Catherine Nultz (Nolty, Nolte, or Nult) in 1736 in the Lancaster area. She was born about 1712 in Muttersholtz, Alsace and because of her age, it appears she moved with her parents to Lancaster in 1717 when she was around 5 years old. Her father was Philip Nult and her mother was Eva Musselman. I have no record to connect her to the Henry Musselman family who had property near Antonius Knussli's property, but it is likely that she was part of that family line when they moved to America. The Musselman family were also of Mennonite background and while the current Musselman company was not founded until 1907, it is most likely linked to the original Musselman family who moved into the Lancaster area in 1717 with the Knussli family and many other Mennonites. Musselman Apple Butter is well known in the grocery stores and if you have ever been to Lancaster you will find it is a custom that a standard serving of cottage cheese goes well topped with apple butter. The link to this line, if proved, would make any descendant of this line a descendant of the Musselman family as well. There are most likely records in the Lancaster Mennonite Historical Society that could prove this link. George and Catherine had 6 children, 3 males and 3 females. They will be shown below in the descendant listing as 2nd generation of this line and the 3rd generations listed are grandchildren. George died on October 19, 1785 in Manheim Twp., Lancaster Co., PA and Catherine died in 1755 at the same location. George did not remarry after Catherine's death.

There is a tremendous amount of history on this family line. It takes 83 pages to print a full narrative register report with all the notes on all of their descendants. There are 182 different family Surnames in the descendant list and there are 4 different spellings of the Knusli name. It takes 21 pages to print out a list of all the descendants of George and his wife. While the first 2 generations of this family remained in PA for the most part, later descendants would spread to at least 23 of the US States plus Canada.

1-George H. KNEISLEY (4 September 1711-19 October 1785)
+Catherine NULTZ (NOLTE) (about 1712-1755)
.....2-Samuel KNEISLY (circa 1738-1803)
.....+Unknown UNKNOWN (circa 1751-before 1841)
........3-Samuel KNEISLY (circa 1771-1814)
.....2-John KNEISLY Sr. (circa 1740-13 December 1811)
.....+Elizabeth UNKNOWN (circa 1741-before 1831)
........3-John KNEISLY Jr. (circa 1761-circa 1822)
........3-George KNEISLY (circa 1763-about 1813)
........3-Samuel KNEISLY (circa 1765-before 1855)
........3-Elizabeth KNEISLY (circa 1780-before 1870)
.....+Magdalena MILLER (circa 1775-before 1865)
........3-Abraham KNEISLEY (12 May 1800-before 1890)
.....2-Catherine KNEISLY (circa 1742-before 1830)
.....+Henry YORDEY (1750-before 1840)
........3-John YORDEY (circa 1771-after 30 September 1843)
........3-Mary YORDEY (circa 1773-before 1863)
........3-Magdalena YORDEY (circa 1775-before 1865)
........3-Peter YORDEY (circa 1777-before 1867)
........3-David YORDEY (circa 1779-before 1869)
........3-Samuel YORDEY (circa 1781-before 1871)
........3-Christian YORDEY (circa 1783-before 1873)
.....2-Barbara KNEISLY (circa 1746-before 1830)
.....+Jacob BEIDLER (circa 1742-1770)
........3-Anna BEIDLER (circa 1769-before 1859)
........3-John BEIDLER (circa 1771-before 1861)

....+Frederick BERG (circa 1741-8 April 1803)
........3-Frederick BERG (circa 1772-August 1804)
........3-David BERG (circa 1774-before 1864)
........3-Barbara BERG (circa 1776-before 1866)
........3-Benjamin BERG (circa 1778-before 1868)
........3-Andrew BERG (circa 1780-before 1870)
........3-Mary BERG (circa 1782-before 1872)
........3-Veronica BERG (circa 1785-before 1875)
....2-Mary KNEISLY (1750-before 1830)
....+John MAYER (circa 1749-before 1839)
....2-George KNEISLY (2 August 1751-20 February 1816)
....+Mary MEYERS (about 1755-before 1794)
........3-Catherine KNEISLY (24 January 1783-4 October 1831)
........3-Daniel KNEISLY (19 October 1785-30 November 1865)
........3-Samuel KNEISLY (circa 1786-August 1830)
........3-Abraham KNEISLY (10 January 1788-22 March 1822)
........3-George KNEISLY (14 September 1789-11 May 1851)
........3-John KNEISLY (11 January 1792-25 November 1868)
....+Elizabeth FURRY (about 1751-before 1841)

There are certain members of this line that I will cover in a later chapter. I will do this for each line to highlight people of note or stories of interest. The following descendants of this line, John Kneisly, George G. Kneisly, Benjamin Franklin Kneisly, and Harry Loren Kneisly are people of note or with interesting stories.

Adam Kneisle (1730 – 1826)

This child was Antonius's 12th child and 5th son. However, this son was born to Elizabeth Yeager and not Magdalena. There was a census taken in 1732 in Hempfield Twp. showing Antoni Knisely, with a birth year of 1657 living with a wife and young child. Antonius was 75 years old at the time and the birth year matches Antonius. Family records indicated Adam's father was Anthony Kneisle, his mother was Elizabeth Yeager and family information indicated Adam's father was Anthony Kneisle who was the first of his line to come to America. Elizabeth was approximately 19 years old in 1732 at the time of the census. Magdalena was still Antonius's wife when he died in 1733 and there was a note in the records of his family history stating "He may have also had another wife." Since my DNA matches up with at least one male individual from each of the other male lines of Antonius's sons and since Adam used Kneisle as his last name, I feel confident in saying that Adam was the son of Antonius Kristopher Knussli. We could not locate any other Anthony in any of the records that would have matched up as being Adam's father. This line is my family line and Adam was my 4th Great Grandfather. The 1730 birth date was from Adam's family history and from Adam's tombstone and compliments the Census taken in Hempfield Twp. in 1732 where there was a young child living with Antonius.

Adam married Elizabeth Eichart, who was born in 1735. We do not have an exact date on this marriage but the date was most likely before Adam's oldest son Anthony was born in 1758 in East Hempfield Twp. Anthony's birth date was taken from his tombstone in the Keltz Cemetery in Ligonier Twp. where both Adam and his first son Anthony are buried. The fact that Adam named his first son Anthony also is a sign that Anthony was Adam's father, since it was typical in those days to name the first son after the father's father. Adam and Elizabeth had 8 children, 3 sons and 5 daughters. All of the children except Anthony were born in Ligonier Twp, Westmoreland Co., PA. Adam was a Conestoga wagon driver and worked and lived in the Lancaster area until the age of 28 when he became a part of the large group of Mennonites and farmers from Lancaster that were asked to use their wagons to haul goods on the Forbes Road to Fort Ligonier in 1758. This was part of the French and Indian War and numerous wagons were needed to supply the large number of British troops who moved into Fort Ligonier in the year of 1758. This army contained around 6,000 soldiers at the peak of the war. Many of the wagon drivers who brought goods to the Fort were given property along the Forbes Trail for their service to Britain and some were asked to move close to the Fort to start farming They were asked to supply fresh food for the troops at both Ligonier and Pittsburgh and as a result many of them moved here early to start farming. We believe Adam moved his family to this area in circa 1761 and moved onto his 1,200 acre

Grant of land that was supplied by General Arthur St. Clair. Fort Ligonier was an active fort that required supplies until it was decommissioned from active status in 1766, and we believe Adam and many of his neighbors were bringing supplies to the soldiers at the fort.

Following is a list of the first three generations of Adam and Elizabeth Eichart Nicely family. You will note below the descendants of Jacob Nicely are included and the change in the surnames. These family members were the result of the capture of Jacob and his being raised as a Native American. This information and several other stories will follow later in the book.

1-Adam NICELY Sr. (1730-1826)
+Elizabeth EICHERT (1735-1829)
....2-Anthony NICELY Sr. (1758-4 December 1845)
....+Sarah Salome HARGNETT (about 1759-about 1849)
........3-Anthony Wayne NICELY (2 August 1806-3 June 1891)
........3-George NICELY (21 March 1810-14 June 1867)
........3-Eliza May "Mary" NICELY (21 Mar. 1810-13 Mar. 1893)
........3-Elizabeth NICELY (5 March 1810-1 July 1878)
........3-Adam NICELY IV (25 Nov. 1812-6 September 1868)
....2-Rosanna NICELY (about 1763-before 1844)
....+William E. KARNS (KERNS) (about 1763-1838)
........3-Adam KARNS (KERN) (about 1810-before 1890)
....2-Adam NICELY Jr. (about 1764-circa May 1838)
....+Mary Sarah? UNKNOWN (22 February 1778-1 August 1819)
........3-Margaret NICELY (1800-1884)
........3-Adam NICELY III (about 1801-before 1891)
........3-Elizabeth NICELY (about 1802-before 1882)
........3-John Fuller "Sawdust" NICELY (3 May 1803-24 June 1845)
........3-Rosanna NICELY (about 1804-1892)
........3-George A. NICELY Sr. (11 May 1805-14 August 1883)
........3-Jacob NICELY (1809-before 1899)
........3-Martha NICELY (1810-before 1890)
....+Esther SCHEIRY (SHIREY) (1801-before 1881)
........3-Catharine "Kathern" NICELY (10 Jun. 1821-27 Aug. 1901)
........3-Susanna NICELY (1822-before 1902)
........3-Anthony A. NICELY (26 June 1827-11 January 1908)

........3-Philip NICELY (9 April 1830-29 May 1866)
........3-David NICELY (9 April 1830-before 1840)
........3-Loweisanna A. "Louisa" NICELY (19 Aug. 1832-13 Dec. 1910)
........3-William NICELY (24 July 1834-25 November 1863)
........3-Henry "Heinrich" NICELY (23 June 1837-17 Nov. 1863)
....2-Mary Elizabeth "Polly" NICELY (1765-1836)
....+Joseph "John" KARNS (KERUENS) (1755-1815)
....2-Catherine NICELY (about 1766-before 1846)
....+John PIPER (about 1765-before 1845)
....2-Jacob "Tsu-Ka-We or Crow" NICELY (22 May 1770-1833)
....+Unknown UNKNOWN (WYNDOT INDIAN) (ca. 1786-bef. 1866)
........3-Jacob "White Crow" WHITECROW (1814-4 May 1876)
........3-Jerry CROW (1815-22 November 1902)
....+Unknown SPICER (about 1810-before 1900)
....+Unknown UNKNOWN (about 1786-before 1866)
........3-Moses CROW (circa 1817-about 1861)
........3-Cah-Quee-Nah CROW (circa 1818-before 1903)
....+Unknown UNKNOWN (about 1785-before 1865)
........3-Wah-Deh-Dhyo-Do-Quah CROW (ca. 1819-bef. 1895)
........3-Cah-Tee-Lih CROW (circa 1821-before 1890)
....2-Margaretha "Margaret" NICELY (10 June 1784-6 Sep. 1854)
....+John George AMBROSE (7 May 1778-11 March 1851)
........3-Margaret AMBROSE (20 Dec. 1804-24 Dec. 1874)
........3-Frederick AMBROSE (about 1805-about 1860)
........3-Elizabeth AMBROSE (about 1806-before 1885)
........3-Mary AMBROSE (14 September 1810-28 May 1882)
........3-Catherine AMBROSE (about 1814-before 1904)
........3-Louise AMBROSE (5 August 1817-14 March 1849)
........3-Sarah AMBROSE (29 April 1821-2 April 1849)
....2-Ann Elizabeth NICELY (29 October 1786-before 1866)
....+Michael MILLER (about 1795-before 1875)

There are certain members of this line that I will cover in a later chapter. I will do this for each line to highlight people of note or stories of interest. Since this is my ancestral line, I have a lot more individual history's to report. The following descendants of this line are, Anthony Nicely Sr., Adam Nicely Jr., Jacob "Crow" Nicely, Matthew Gelvin Burkholder Sr., Josiah and David Nicely, Frederick

Rankin Nicely Sr., Dr. Robert Francis Nicely Sr., Dr. William W. McKenna, William Elder Nicely, Ronald Earl Nicely (the author), John Robert Nicely, Dr. Robert Francis Nicely Jr., Donald Arthur Gilmore, Todd Garrett Pelky, and Adam Brett Nicely all who are people of note or with interesting stories.

CHAPTER EIGHT

1739 Knusli Line

Elias Abraham Knisely (1683 – 1762)

As I mentioned in an earlier chapter, I was contacted, several years ago by a Knisely descendant who had an entirely different ancestor line. This line immigrated to America in 1739 and settled in York County, PA. A male member of this line agreed to take a Y-DNA 12 test and when the test was returned, it was an exact match with my Y-DNA. This means that this line came from a different person than our earliest known ancestor Hans Knussli. Hans had a son who stayed in Berne when he left, but I was not able to link this son or any of his descendants to any of the members in the 1739 line. The 1739 line's earliest ancestor was Elias Abraham Knisely who was born on April 14, 1683 in the Canton of Berne in Switzerland. This name could not be found among any of the descendants of Johannes "Hans" Knussli, who was the son of our Hans Knussli. This means that the 1739 line had to be a descendant of an earlier ancestor or perhaps a brother of our Hans. This will be a mystery for now and perhaps into the future, when we learn more about our Switzerland ancestors and be able to make a link. So for now we will assume this line came from a brother or a cousin of our Hans Knussli.

Elias Abraham Knisely was born on April 1683 in the Canton of Bern Switzerland and died on September 28, 1762 in Cologne, Germany and was married to Annatarcia Swigart on October 22, 1705 in the Canton of Berne. She was born on September 12, 1687 in the Canton of Berne in Switzerland and died on October 18, 1761 in Cologne, Germany. They had 10 children, 7 males and 3 females. Their oldest son, Nicholas E. Knisely, was born on August 16, 1706 and moved to America in 1739, where he died on November 14, 1781 in York County, PA. I have the names and a birth date of all of Elias's other children, but there is no current information showing if they moved to America and no firm death dates or location is indicated. So for the current time and until new research indicates differently, the descendants of the 1739 line were all descendants of Nicholas E. Knisely.

There is only a modest amount of history on this line and the list shown below is a 5 generation descendant report. The one line where we have a lot of information was a 4th generation member by the name of John Knisely Sr. He was a Grandson of Nicholas Knisely. A complete register report on this line starting with Elias Knisely would cover only 28 pages and the major portion of the report would be the John Knisely Sr. section. There are 61 different Surnames in the descendant list and there are 5 different spellings of the Knusli name. This line has spread out to at least 5 different states.

1-Elias Abraham KNISELY (14 April 1683-28 September 1762)
+Annatarcia SWIGART (12 September 1687-18 October 1761)
....2-Nicholas E. KNISELY (16 August 1706-14 November 1781)
....+Anna Belle NURENBERG (22 Sep. 1709-22 October 1783)
........3-Anthony KNISELY (7 March 1728-19 March 1799)
........+Mary SNYDER (circa 1729-before 1790)
........+Catherine Elizabeth "Rudy" PRESSEL (6 May 1747-before 1837)
............4-Solomon Sylvester KNISELY (10 July 1793-26 January 1865)
............+Elizabeth RUBY (circa 1799-before 1889)
................5-David KNISELY (1819-1909)
................5-Anthony KNISELY (1821-1876)
................5-Catherine KNISELY (1823-1878)
................5-Daniel KNISELY (1826-1913)
................5-Joseph KNISELY (1828-1883)
................5-John KNISELY (17 Apr. 1830-25 Dec. 1895)
................5-Mary Ann KNISELY (1835-1862)
................5-Elizabeth KNISELY (1837-1883)
................5-Susan Jane KNISELY (1841-1862)
................5-Barbara Lacy KNISELY (1845-1902)
............4-Susan Jane KNEISLEY (6 Feb. 1796-before 1886)
........3-Samuel KNISELY (23 April 1730-19 March 1799)
........+Unknown UNKNOWN (circa 1731-before 1821)
............4-John KNISELY Sr. (21 Sep. 1752-21 Dec. 1834)
............+Mary "Elizabeth?" MILLER (21 Sep. 1757-before 1847)
................5-George KNEISLY (about 1777-1819)
................5-Abraham KNISELY (16 Feb. 1778-28 Dec. 1841)

...............5-Salome Sarah KNISELY (16 Nov. 1780-16 Nov. 1820)
...............5-John KNISELY Jr. (27 August 1782-before 1830)
...............5-Samuel A. KNISELEY (Nov. 1784-2 June 1867)
...............5-Elizabeth KNISELY (11 Nov. 1787-11 Mar.1867)
...............5-Jacob KNISELY (15 Feb. 1789-15 Feb. 1833)
...............5-David Peter KNISELY (8 July 1792-4 Sep. 1877)
...............5-Joseph KNISELY (1795-17 April 1882)
...............5-Mary KNISELY (19 Feb. 1796-3 Feb.1874)
...............5-Susan KNISELY (1797-before 1887)
........3-Solomon KNISELY (14 September 1733-before 1823)
........3-Susanna KNISELY (18 October 1736-before 1826)
........3-James KNISELY (13 February 1738-29 April 1790)
........3-Mary Anna Belle KNISELY (16 May 1748-before 1838)
....2-John W. KNISELY (2 November 1708-1757)
....2-Mary Ann KNISELY (18 October 1710-before 1800)
....2-George KNISELY (27 March 1712-1785)
....2-Abraham KNISELY (7 July 1714-before 1804)
....2-Susan KNISELY (22 May 1716-before 1806)
....2-Eva Dion KNISELY (18 September 1718-before 1808)
....2-Samuel KNISELY (3 April 1720-before 1810)
....2-Anthony KNISELY (14 June 1722-before 1812)
....2-Solomon Sylvester KNISELY (9 July 1724-before 1814)

John Knisely Sr. (1752 – 1834)

John Knisely Sr. (Samuel Knisely-3, Nicolas E. Knisely-2, Elias Abraham Knisely-1)

John was part of an interesting story in this line. John was the son of Samuel and an Unknown Knisely, born on September 21, 1752 in York Co., PA and died on December 21, 1834 in New Philadelphia, OH, where he was considered the Father of New Philadelphia. He married Mary Miller on November 10, 1777. She was born on September 21, 1757 and died on April 16, 1822 in New Philadelphia.. This was a marriage between descendants of the 1717 line and the 1739 line. Mary Miller (David Miller-3, Barbara Kneisley-2, Antonius Kristopher Knussli-1) was a Great Granddaughter of Antonius Kristopher Knussli (Immigrated 1717) and John was a Grandson of Nicholas E. Knisely (Immigrated 1739). This is the first link between the two families, who were likely linked somewhere in Berne Switzerland, where both lines were located. I have not found any other links in the US, but there is a high probability of another link somewhere in the history of both lines.

John and Mary lived in York for a number of years and then in 1795 they moved to Bedford Co. in PA., where they set up a grist mill and a hostelry. The first 8 of their children were most likely born in York County and the remaining 3 were born in Bedford County, based on their dates of birth. The records show that John was very successful in his business opportunities with income sometimes amounting to $1,000 a week. The town of Bedford was located around the fort named Fort Bedford that was built by the British Army as a supply location, along the Forbes Trail that was used by General Forbes and the British Army to attack the French at Fort Duquesne. Then they continued the trail to Fort Ligonier about 50 miles further west of Bedford. The French Fort at Pittsburgh was eventually captured by General Forbes and his Army, with the name of Fort Duquesne being changed to Fort Pitt in 1758, the fort at Bedford and the fort in Ligonier became supply depots, and the Forbes Road became a main route to supply the Forts from Bedford to Pittsburgh. Large numbers of Conestoga wagons delivered goods along this route as well as drovers driving animals to the west. Within a few short years, it became the main route for people moving to the west. My Adam Nicely family traveled along this route in 1761 and moved to a piece of land outside of Fort Ligonier. The flowing traffic on this road past Bedford was probably the main reason for John's business success in Bedford. In 1803, John and his son Samuel decided to go on a hunting trip to Ohio, which was now reasonably safe from Indian uprisings. He met up with a friendly Indian group and used them as guides to take them to an area where deer were known to be located. During his trip, he found a nice spot along a river that would make a nice site for a town and decided to purchase the land. When fall arrived he left his son, and his arms and supplies, with the Indians, traveled back to Bedford, sold his grist mill, hostelry, and farm for $16,000, went to the seat of government, and negotiated for 3,554 acres of land in one tract in Ohio. He then gathered up his belongings and prepared to move with his wife and 10 children to his new property. He also persuaded 33 other individuals to join in this venture and they started west in the spring of 1804.

When he got settled in his new home, he began to lay out a town that was patterned after the checkerboard square pattern of Philadelphia, PA and named many of the streets the same as the names in Philadelphia. It was through his efforts that the town grew and prospered. The town was known by all the townspeople as Knisely Town against John's wishes until finally, at his insistence, the town took the name of New Philadelphia and eventually became the county seat of Tuscarawas County. He donated the land for the courthouse and 100 lots and 160 outlaying acres that were sold to offset the cost of building the new courthouse. He was truly the Founding Father of New Philadelphia and his grave site is in the East Fair Street Cemetery where his tombstone reads "John Knisely, The Founder of New Philadelphia"

The town of New Philadelphia in 2011 had a population of 17,287 people. Following is a list of some of the noted residents of New Philadelphia.

A. Victor Donahey (Ohio Governor and US Senator.)
Cie Grant (Football player for the New Orleans Saints)
William Donahey (Illustrator, The Teenie Weenies)
Norman Bel Geddes (Industrial Engineer)
Woody Hayes (Football coach Ohio State University)
Dave Leggett (Football Player for the Chicago Cardinals)
John Mackey (American Composer)
Bill Moffit (American Composer)

John was a large contributor to the success of this town and a part of our Knusli family history. Following is a 3 generation descendant list of his family line.

1-John KNISELY Sr. (21 September 1752-21 December 1834)
+Mary "Elizabeth?" MILLER (21 September 1757-16 April 1822)
....2-George KNEISLY (about 1777-1819)
....2-Abraham KNISELY (16 February 1778-28 December 1841)
....+Racheal WOLF (22 September 1782-27 April 1823)
........3-Reuben KNISELY (1807-before 1880)
........3-Joseph Perry KNISELY (28 August 1817-before 1907)
....2-Salome Sarah KNISELY (16 Nov. 1780-16 Nov. 1820)
....+Philip MINNICH (4 September 1772-4 September 1824)

....2-John KNISELY Jr. (27 August 1782-before 1830)
....+Mary WOLF (1 January 1778-before 1858)
........3-William KNISELY (about 1801-before 1891)
........3-Christian KNISELY (about 1803-before 1893)
........3-Sarah KNISELY (about 1805-before 1895)
........3-Nancy KNISELY (about 1807-before 1897)
........3-Andrew KNISELY (15 Nov. 1813-16 October 1872)
....2-Samuel A. KNISELEY (November 1784-2 June 1867)
....+Sarah Elizabeth SHANKS (1 April 1792-18 October 1857)
........3-Elizabeth KNISELY (20 January 1817-before 1907)
........3-Urius C. KNISELY (10 September 1818-10 May 1875)
........3-Rebecca KNISELY (14 February 1820-before 1910)
........3-Suzanna KNISELY (20 January 1822-before 1912)
........3-John B. KNISELY (20 January 1822-before 1912)
........3-Hannah KNISELY (9 April 1824-before 1914)
........3-Mary Jane KNISELEY (1 April 1826-before 1916)
........3-Jacob B. KNISELY (1828-before 1918)
........3-Samuel Stough KNISELY (16 April 1832-before 1922)
........3-William KNISELY (15 April 1833-before 1923)
........3-George W. KNISELY (10 November 1835-before 1925)
........3-Paul W. KNISELY (26 September 1838-before 1928)
....2-Elizabeth KNISELY (11 November 1787-11 March 1867)
....2-Jacob KNISELY (15 February 1789-15 February 1833)
....2-David Peter KNISELY (8 July 1792-4 September 1877)
....+Sarah BOWERS (23 October 1792-9 July 1889)
........3-Mary Ann KNISLEY (20 October 1817-14 March 1851)
........3-Elizabeth KNISELY (12 February 1819-16 June 1854)
........3-Sarah KNISELY (18 April 1820-30 April 1895)
........3-Daniel KNISELY (5 November 1821-4 March 1904)
........3-Rebecca KNISELY (25 February 1823-19 June 1902)
........3-Jonas KNISELY (8 October 1824-12 May 1901)
........3-Susan KNISELY (3 February 1826-8 February 1908)
........3-Sabilla KNISELY (5 June 1827-2 July 1918)
........3-David KNISELY (24 February 1829-3 February 1849)
........3-John KNISELY (27 November 1830-26 November 1912)
........3-Solomon KNISELY (19 January 1833-1 March 1833)
........3-Oliver P. KNISELY (4 August 1834-3 April 1911)
....+Emma JOHNSON (about 1793-before 1873)

........3-Caroline A. KNISELY (about 1836-before 1926)
........3-Luther KNISELY (6 May 1837-20 March 1849)
........3-Isaac KNISELY (23 January 1839-before 1929)
....2-Joseph KNISELY (1795-17 April 1882)
....2-Mary KNISELY (19 February 1796-3 February 1874)
....2-Susan KNISELY (1797-before 1887)
....+Samuel STONE (about 1796-before 1876)

Following is a picture of John Knisely's Headstone in New Philadelphia, Ohio. The Cemetery is located next to the Sacred Heart Church located at 139 Third Street in New Philadelphia. As you pass the church, which is on the right side of Third Street, turn to the right onto Fair Street and you will see a small mausoleum on the left side of the street in the cemetery. Just behind the mausoleum along the sidewalk is where his stone is located. His wife Mary Miller is buried with him. As I noted above Mary was the Great Granddaughter of Antonius Kristopher Knussli of Lancaster, PA. The inscription reads: John Knisely, Founder of New Philadelphia, O. in 1804. Died December 15, 1834:, Aged 82 YS. & 3 MS: Also listed Mary His Wife Died April 16, 1822:. Aged 61 YS,. 1 MO. & 22 DS. There is a slight difference on her birth date based on these numbers. I am not sure which is correct.

There are no other stories from this line available to me at the time of this writing in 2013.

CHAPTER NINE

Family Information & Stories From The Johannes Hans Kneisley Sr. Line

Christian Kneisly (1757 – 1836)

Christian Kneisly (Johannes Hans Kneisley Sr. -3, Antonius Kristopher Knussli Sr. -2, Hans Knussli -1).

Christian is the son of Johannes Hans and Mary Christina Secrist Kneisley and appears to be the first of our family to leave the Lancaster area of PA and move to Canada. There were other family members, who also moved to Canada later on. Christian and his wife Anna Steiner moved there some time after the Revolutionary War. Christian fought in the Revolutionary War and his name appears on the Patriot Honor Roll, Memorial Bell Tower at Valley Forge. He was a Private 2nd Class in Captain Duncan's Company, Sixth Battalion of the Lancaster County Militia. It is likely that he purchased the land in Ontario from a British Loyalist soldier, who was offered land for their service by the British Government after the War. Most of these soldiers had no interest in owning land in Canada so they were glad to sell their land for cash. Many of those that purchased land were Quaker or Mennonite.

In a brief History of Mennonites in Ontario by Louis J. Burkholder, "Abraham Neaf obtained a grant of land in 1794 and Benjamin Hersche from Lancaster came in 1795. The Mennonite families spread into Bertie and Humberstone townships along Lake Erie, and Willoughby Township, to the north along the Niagara River. This settlement was also known as "Black Creek" because of the stream by that name which flows through Bertie and empties into the Niagara. Christian died in Humberstone Township indicating that he was a member of the group that settled there.

Christian showed the pioneer spirit of the Knusli family in moving to a new area to gain his own land.

Sen. George Omit Deise (1836 – 1872)

Sen. George Omit Deise (Sarah Quiggle -7, Margaret Rebecca Nicely -6, Christian Kneisly -5, John Hans Kneisly -4, Johannes Hans Kneisley Sr. -3, Antonius Kristopher Knussli Sr. -2, Hans Knussli -1).

George is the son of Joseph B. and Sarah C. Quiggle Deise and was a very active political person within Clinton County in PA during his 35 year life time. He began as a teacher in Wayne Township and then 'read' law under C. A. Mayer, Esq. and was admitted to the bar by 1856. He served as the District Attorney in Clinton Co., PA in 1859 through 1862, then was elected to the position of Pennsylvania State Senator in 1866 and 1867. In February 14, 1870, a court decreed that an incorporated body be established named "The Central Normal School Association of the State of Pennsylvania". George Omet Deise was one of 15 Trustees that met until May 5, 1870 where they accepted a deed of 16 acres donated to the Association by Philip M. Price and where they acknowledged the acquisition of $26,000.00 through subscription, thus funding and establishing the "State Normal School for Lock Haven" now known as Lock Haven University.

He died at age 35 cutting short a promising career in the education and political areas, but still a member of our family who brought honor to the history of the Knusli family.

Thomas Alexander Deise (1899 – 2000)

Thomas Alexander Deise (John Peale Deise -9, George Omet Deise -8, Sarah Quiggle -7, Margaret Rebecca Nicely -6, Christian Kneisly -5, John Hans Kneisly -4, Johannes Hans Kneisley Sr. -3, Antonius Kristopher Knussli Sr. -2, Hans Knussli -1).

Thomas Alexander Deise is the son of John Peale and Ada Lillian Caroline Smith and was a veteran fire-fighter who led efforts to modernize the Sacramento California Fire Department when he was chief. He died of congestive heart failure at 100 years of age. Mr Deise was a labor crew foreman for Southern Pacific railroad when he joined the city Fire Department in 1932. He served as chief from 1957 until his retirement in 1969. Among other things, he was known for the enthusiasm he brought to his work. Right up until his retirement, he frequently appeared at the scene of fires. His long career with the department coincided with its emergence as one of the "best in the state." The Bee, a newspaper, editorialized on November 25, 1969. As chief, the editorial stated, Mr. Deise "carried on the tradition of firefighting excellence which enabled Sacramento to enjoy one of the best safety records in the state." Mr. Deise was married and had no children. The Fire Department was his life, and Mr. Deise made no secret in 1969 newspaper accounts that he was unhappy with the prospect of retirement. But on December 3, 1969, he had reached what was then the mandatory city retirement age of 70 and had no choice but to step down. He was born in Pittsburgh PA and moved to Sacramento when he was a youngster. He attended Sutter Grammar School, graduating in 1914. He attended Sacramento High School but did not graduate. Instead, he went to work for Southern Pacific and then served in the Navy during World War I. After the war, he returned to his railroad job. In a biographical sketch submitted to the Bee in 1969, Mr. Deise said he had once thought of becoming a professional boxer "but soon found out it was too tough a racket." "The most interesting part of my career with the Sacramento Fire Department," he wrote, "is that each day is a continual challenge." He was married for 63 years to the former Helen Hunzijer, who survives. He was a past commander of American Legion Post 61. Subsequent to his death, The Post was renamed the Thomas A. Deise Post #61, and the city renamed the Department Headquarters after him.

This is another well respected and noted member of the Knusli family line.

Melvin Henry Knisely (1904 – 1975)

Melvin Henry Knisely (Samuel Henry Knisely -8, Samuel E. Knisely -7, Christian Knisley -6, Samuel Knisley -5, Christian Kneisly -4, Johannes Hans Kneisley Sr. -3, Antonius Kristopher Knussli Sr. -2, Hans Knussli -1)

Melvin is the son of Samuel Henry and Flora Belle Hagemann Knisely and attended medical school at the University of Chicago with the intent of becoming a doctor. The recession cut short his degree efforts and he settled for a PHD. He became an Assistant Professor of Anatomy at the Medical College and began doing research work. That work led him to writing a brief article that appeared in the June 4, 1940 issue of Life magazine. This article covered his invention of a quartz rod which made blood vessels transparent and three dimensional so they could view blood flowing in the vessels of the body with the use of a microscope. This aided in the research work he was performing on red blood cells as they flowed through the vessels of healthy animals and humans. On one particular occasion, he was examining a monkey who had been infected with malaria and noticed the red blood cells were clumping together in lumps as they floated past his microscope. He and his associates began to study animals and humans with various diseases and injuries. This led to the finding that red cell clumping was associated with over 50 conditions from the common cold to hysteria. They found the cells were stuck together by a protein that apparently came from something in the body to protect the cells. This process was named as blood sludge because it slowed the flow of blood in the veins and arteries. This discovery led to a second article in Life magazine on May 31, 1948.

This discovery and others in the process led to a nomination for the Nobel Prize in 1947 under the name of Melvin Knisley and in 1948 and 1949 under the name of Melvin Knisely. Although he did not win the Nobel Prize, it led to him being offered the position of the Chairman of the Department of Anatomy at the Medical College of South Carolina in Charleston, which he took in late 1948. His PHD had helped him get into and kept him in the medical research business, as well as being a teacher.

He later wrote on article titled "Brain Damage Starts with the First Drink' that appeared in LISTEN, Journal of Better Living, Volume 22, page number 12. This article was an extension of his study on blood sludge since the drinking of alcoholic beverages has the same type of effect on the red blood cells. This sludge is difficult to move through the smaller veins in the brain and leads to loss of brain cells that are irreplaceable. People who consume more alcohol have larger empty cavities around their brain which will lead in the long term to mental illness.

The following information comes from the Wikipedia Encyclopedia.

Melvin Henry Knisely (1904 - 30 March 1975), was an American physiologist who first observed the pathological clumping of red and white cells, in vivo, at the capillary level. One of the most cited Knisely works was his research which documented the fact that even one drink kills brain cells, which are irreplaceable.

In 1948, Knisely was nominated for a Nobel Prize by his mentor August Krogh, the 1920 Nobel Laureate winner for physiology and medicine. Knisely's positions included a term as chairman of the Department of Anatomy at the Medical College of South Carolina (1948-1974).

In 1983 The International Society on Oxygen Transport to Tissue established the Melvin H. Knisely Award to honor Knisely's accomplishments in the field of the transport of oxygen and other metabolites and anabolites in the human body.

You can find other information on this individual by doing a search on the internet.

This was a lifelong work for Melvin and his efforts led to advances in the analysis and treatment of many illnesses. He is truly an honorable and memorable member of the Knusli family.

Jacob Clarence (Jake) Knisely (1936 -)

Jacob Clarence (Jake) Knisely (Robert William Knisely -10, Jacob Clarence Knisely -9, Joseph Elsworth Kniseley -8, Solomon Kniseley -7, Daniel Kniseley -6, John Samuel Knisely -5, Anthony Kneisly Sr. -4, Johannes Hans Kneisley -3, Antonius Kristopher Knussli Sr. -2, Hans Knussli -1).

Jake is the son of Robert William and Doris Lucina Swineford Knisely. Jake and his wife Sondra played a major part in the connection of the Nicely family line from Ligonier, PA and the Whitecrow family line from Grove, Oklahoma, who were descendants of Jacob Nicely who was captured in 1775 in Ligonier as a young boy. Jake was contacted in 2001 by the Whitecrow family and then in 2003 he contacted Ronald Nicely from the Ligonier line. The meeting in 2003, led to the connection of the two separated families. The information shared at this meeting and in subsequent conversations led to the writing of the book "The Indian Capture Of Jacob (Kneisle) Nicely" and to DNA testing of Jake and Ron Nicely. I would point to this as the break through that brought about resurgence in the history of our Knusli family. Jake was contacted by the Whitecrow family by letter searching for a Jacob Knisely that might be a relative of the captured boy Jacob. Jake had a large history file on his family lines and a strong interest in genealogy that drove him and his wife to visit with the Whitecrow family and attempt to make a connection. When that failed, his research brought him to Westmoreland County. The Whitecrow family urged him to search in Westmoreland County because they had a reference to a place named Loyal Hanna in PA and they had located the Loyalhanna Creek, located in Westmoreland County. In 2003, through Jake and Sondra's efforts, they were able to locate Ron Nicely (the author) and that led to the connection of the two branches. At the time of our meeting in 2003, I had just shy of 1,000 names in my file and today after 10 more years of research and people reading the book and contacting me, there are over 12,000 Knusli descendants in my genealogy file and over 34,000 names of connected or collateral lines to our Knusli family. The importance of Jake and Sondra's efforts cannot be ignored and they should be honored for the efforts they made. Their contact with me drove me to do further research and to not only connect the Whitecrow and Ligonier Nicely family lines, but also DNA testing with Jake and I that established a link of the Ligonier Nicely line to Antonius Kristopher Knussli as our common ancestor and the ancestor who was the first of our line to move to America..

The Knusli family owes a debt of gratitude and respect to Jake and Sondra for their efforts in helping to bring the families together. Their efforts were a great contribution to the history of our family. Jake said to me several times, "The day I met you and connected you to the Whitecrows, your life changed big time." It's true because of him, I extended my research and have gone way beyond my original expectations of knowing more about my line which now led to writing two books on the family.

Robert August Knisely (1939 -)

Robert August Knisely (Melvin Henry Knisely -9, Samuel Henry Knisely -8, Samuel E. Knisely -7, Christian Knisely -6, Samuel Knisley -5, Christian Kneisly -4, Johannes Hans Kneisley -3, Antonius Kristopher Knussli Sr. -2, Hans Knussli -1)

Robert Knisely is the son of Melvin Henry and Violetta Butzer Knisely. He is an Adjunct Professor at Johns Hopkins University and has had a long history of work in the government in Washington DC. He was educated at the Georgetown University Law Center in DC. He has consistently been called upon for high-pressure, short-deadline special efforts in a wide variety of federal programs. President Ford's Clemency Board, the energy crisis, and Vice President Gore's National Performance Review represent only a partial summary of his ubiquitous presence when a new issue is being faced and a volunteer executive to manage it is needed.

As an attorney, he has spent thirty years in the American civil service, twenty of them as a senior executive. His career spanned seven cabinet departments and an additional seven agencies and special projects. He has brought real progress through the thickets of Washington. He has been on the Management and Governance Team of the Innovations in American Government Program at the Kennedy School of Government at Harvard University for eight years.

He has taught at both the high school level (the St. Albans School in Washington) and the graduate school level (Institute for Policy Studies at Johns Hopkins University). He has owned 110 acres in West Virginia's Lost River Valley since 1968, and has been a member of the board of the Cacapon Institute and Board President.

Robert is another outstanding member of this family line and is listed in the Who's Who of America.

Rev. Harry Lee Knisely (1940 -)

Rev. Harry Lee Knisely (Harry Knisely -9, William Benton Knisely -8, John Knisely -7, George Michael Kniseley -6, John Samuel Knisely -5, Anthony Kneisly Sr. -4, Johannes Hans Kneisley -3, Antonius Kristopher Knussli Sr. -2, Hans Knussli -1)

The Rev. Harry Lee Knisely is the son of the late Harry and Ada Mae Lee Knisely. His first calling in life was to teach, and to that end he earned a Bachelor's Degree with a major in Theology and Philosophy from Juniata College in 1963. He began to teach immediately in the Chambersburg Area School District in the areas of French and Speed Reading. During the years from 1963 to 1965, he completed his Master's Degree in Education at Shippensburg University in 1965 with a concentration in reading and administration. During that time of his life, he followed the call of God into the Episcopal Church. He was confirmed at St. Stephen's Cathedral in Harrisburg by The Rt. Rev. John Thomas Heistand. Several years ago, he learned that he was a distant cousin through Antonius Knusli's wife Magdalena Hempstead (Heistand). In September of 1965, he followed his second call in life and began the discernment process leading to his ordination into the ordained ministry of the Episcopal Church. He matriculated at Yale University Divinity School and in 1969 graduated with a Bachelor's of Sacred Theology degree with honors. That degree was later declared by the University as a Master's Degree in Theology.

On June 14, 1969, he was ordained to the Sacred Order of Deacons, and then on December 7, 1969, he was ordained to the Sacred Order of Priests at St. Mary's Church, Williamsport, in the Diocese of Harrisburg. Over the next thirty-one years, he served six dioceses and several congregations.

In December 2000, he retired from the full time ordained ministry, and he and his wife of forty-seven years moved to Central Pennsylvania. Living in Carlisle ever since, he continues to work as needed there in various congregations and around the diocese. Over all these years, he has had a leadership role in an annual Knisely Reunion, held the last Sunday in July at Memorial Park in

Claysburg. This site is just north of Bedford, PA, and this July they will gather for our 85th time.

He has been a spiritual influence on our family and has followed the religious belief of our Mennonite ancestors. He is a worthy and honorable member of the Knusli line.

Michael Douglas Nicely Sr. (1945 -)

Michael Douglas Nicely (Henson Ballard Nicely -10, Henson Nicely -9, Henry Clay Nicely -8, James A. Nicely -7, Jonas (John) Niceley -6, Samuel Kneisly -5, Anthony Kneisly Sr. -4, Johannes Hans Kneisley -3, Antonius Kristopher Knussli Sr. -2, Hans Knussli -1).

Michael Douglas Nicely is the son of Henson Ballard and Gloria McCooley Nicely. We were able to connect Michael to his father and this family line by Y-DNA testing. I am including his interesting story here to show the success that can be accomplished using DNA testing. Michael's wife Anna had a chance meeting with a relative of mine through my Grandmother Elder's family. She noticed Anna's last name of Nicely and asked if she knew me and ended up giving Anna the information to reach me. Michael had been a child of a WWII hurried up marriage between his mother Gloria and his father Henson Nicely as he headed off to war. When the war ended and his father, mother and now Michael, who was born after his father had went to war, got back together and settled. However, the love that existed before he went off to war was no longer there and conflict began that led to a separation and divorce. As his father left, in anger, his mother told Henson that Michael was not his son. For over 60 years, Michael was told by his mother that his dad was Henson and Henson was told this also but he never believed Michael's mother Gloria. During the intervening years, there was limited contact between Michael and Henson and he was raised by his mother with her 2nd husband.

When Anna got in touch with me, she wondered if I could locate Michael's ancestors and establish his tree. She also asked if there was any way to prove Henson was Michael's father. I explained that a Y-DNA test by Michael would be the first step. If his Y-DNA matched mine, then his father would have the same DNA and Henson would be a member of the Knusli line. I suggested if the test was confirmed, they could take the information to Henson and perhaps convince him to meet with Michael. The test results showed an exact match and confirmed his father was Henson. It took a few months to convince Henson that Michael was his son but soon they began to talk and they had some nice conversations. They were finally able to meet in WV at Henson's home and were able to spend 2 days visiting. While at the meeting, the sister of Henson's wife and her husband came to visit and Henson introduced Mike to them as his son. It was a major moment for Mike. After that visit, Mike and Henson were able to talk by phone about every two weeks. Mike sent Henson pictures of his children and grandchildren, so Henson could see his descendants. Then Henson's wife died and he moved in with his wife's sister and just recently, Henson died.

This was an exciting time for all concerned and an emotional finish to an over 60 year separation of father and son. The Y-DNA test between Jake Knisely and myself established the basis for this connection, since Jake, Henson and Mike are all descendants of the same family line.

Alexander (Alex) Knisely (1954 -)

Alexander (Alex) Knisely (Samuel Emerson Knisely -9, Samuel Henry Knisely -8, Samuel E. Knisely -7, Christian Knisley -6, Samuel Knisley -5, Christian Kneisly -4, Johannes Hans Kneisley Sr. -3, Antonius Kristopher Knussli Sr. -2, Hans Knussli -1).

Alex Knisely is the son of Samuel Emerson and Kris Sandburg MD Knisely. He was trained as a physician and failed as a surgeon. He then moved into pathology (the study of how disease affects organs and tissues), especially the pathology of children -- pediatric pathology -- and took an interest in disorders that affect the infant liver. This in turn brought him into contact with geneticists and physiologists who wanted to study cell lines and observations that he had collected, particularly among the Pennsylvania, Ohio, and Indiana Amish. In reading Amish families' books of ancestry, he was delighted to learn that a few Knisely's, as well as wheelbarrow loads full of Nissly's and Nissley's, were to be found! His career saw him moving from Pittsburgh to London and then to Hungary which is a grand example of Knusli attitude of "Take a chance. It will work out somehow." It is that attitude that brought the first of our forefathers across the ocean to America. His skills, good luck, and persistence let him take part in defining, with geneticists and physiologists, some newly recognized forms of liver disease in childhood and in ferreting out some aspects of how the liver works, not only in disease but also in health, doing all of this while having fun within his chosen occupation. He is currently connected to the Institute of Liver Studies / Histopathology at King's College Hospital in London., UK. He is part of the circle of life going back to London, where our family left on the long ship journey to America.

Alex is a member of our family, who showed the strength of our family when faced with failure in one area but moved on to success in another area and brings honor to the Knisely (Knusli) family name.

Dr. Jonathan Petrus Sandberg Knisely MD (1958 -)

Dr. Jonathan P. Knisely MD (Samuel Emerson Knisely -9, Samuel Henry Knisely -8, Samuel E. Knisely -7, Christian Knisely -6, Samuel Knisley -5, Christian Kneisly -4, Johannes Hans Kneisley -3, Antonius Kristopher Knussli Sr. -2, Hans Knussli -1)

Dr. Jonathan Knisely MD is the son of Samuel Emerson and Kris Sandburg MD Knisely. He has served as an MD for over 27 years. His medical education was at the University of Pennsylvania in Philadelphia, PA. He is currently employed at the North Shore University Hospital as Chief and Co-Director for Radiosurgery and Stereotactic Radiation Therapy, Radiation Medicine and is an Associate Professor, Radiation Medicine. His prior employment was at the Yale University School of Medicine and Yale Cancer Center, New Haven, CT. He has written papers and does speaking engagements on his specialty.

Jonathan is another well respected member of the Knusli line of descendants and is listed in the Who's Who of America.

CHAPTER TEN

Family Information & Stories From The Antonius Kristopher (Anthony) Kneussel Jr. Line

Jonas (John) Kniceley Sr. (1769 – 1817)

Jonas (John) Kniceley Sr. (Michael Kniceley -4, Antonius Kristopher "Anthony" Kneussel Jr. -3, Antonius Kristopher Knussli Sr. -2, Hans Knussli -1).

Jonas is the son of Michael and Catherine Unknown Kniceley. He was an early pioneer in Tennessee. He was born in Washington Co., VA and he died in Grainger Co., TN. Jonas had purchased land in Sullivan Co., NC which later became Sullivan Co., TN. In 1814, Jonas sold this property and purchased 127.5 acres from Bolsur Shirley in Granger Co., TN. He served in the 4th Regiment (Boyd's) Virginia Militia, in the War of 1812. After serving his appointed six months, he was given a land grant, which was probably the land he owned in Grainger Co., TN. He purchased the 127.5 acres for $50.00 so it is assumed it was part of the grant process.

He was married about 1799 and had 2 children to an unknown wife, who died young. In 1802, he married Katherine Grubb and they had 9 more children from 1803 until 1816. At the age of 47, he and Katherine, and the 11 children loaded up their wagon and traveled to his newly purchased land. He had great plans for the rundown property he purchased. After they got settled in the little shack that was located on the property, he needed to go to the nearest town and purchase a milk cow and some other animals for the farm. It was about 50 to 55 miles away and he left Katherine with the children and indicated he would be gone for perhaps 2 weeks. Unfortunately, he did not return and after 3 to 4 weeks, Katherine asked a friend of the family to follow his trail to see if they could find him. About halfway to his destination, his horse must have slipped and fell down an embankment, and the horse landed saddle first on Jonas's chest. The family friend carried what was left of his body home to be buried near his family. There is no record of where he was buried. The horse had apparently broken its leg in the fall and Jonas before he died had shot the horse to put him out of his misery. His hopes and dreams died with him and left Katherine to raise the children alone. She raised them through the Civil War that raged all around the area where they lived.

As a side line to this family, the first child and daughter of Jonas and Katherine, Rayjeanah Nicely met with tragedy. She had married John Sparkman in circa 1823. In 1930, Rayjeanah was murdered by arsenic poisoning, presumably by her husband and his girlfriend Elizabeth Ray. John and Elizabeth were indicted for the murder, but in 1832, they were tried and acquitted of the charges. The prosecutor of record for the trial was Jonas Nicely Jr. After the stress of the trial, Katherine decided to move what was left of her family to a place near the village of Liberty Hill, TN.

This story represents some of what many of our early family pioneers faced in their efforts to improve their lives and to raise their families.

Gillon Truett "Gil" Niceley (1923 – 2005)

Gillon James "Jim" Niceley (Dr. Curtis Lafayette Niceley -9, James Buchanan "Whistling Jim" Niceley -8, Wesley Nicely -7, William Nicely -6, Jonas "John" Kniseley Sr. -5, Michael Kniceley -4, Antonius Kristopher "Anthony" Kneussel Jr. -3, Antonius Kristopher Knussli Sr. -2, Hans Knussli -1).

Gil is the son of Dr. Curtis Layfayette and Trailing Arbutus Broome Niceley. Gil was involved in a very important event in the history of World War II. When the Enola Gay, on August 6, 1945, dropped the nuclear bomb on Hiroshima, The Straight Flush was used as the weather patrol aircraft that proceeded the Enola Gay into Japan to gather weather and wind information for the bombing. Gil was the tail gunner in the Straight Flush and had a front row seat to view the explosion as they were flying away from the bombing site. He was part of the crew that was assigned to the plane in April 1945. From June 1945 through July 1945, the plane flew 11 training flights and 6 combat missions over Japan in which they dropped five-ton TNT pumpkin bombs, which had the same handling characteristics as the nuclear weapon. They bombed Tokyo, Otsu, Kanose, and Maizuru with the 5 ton bombs which gave them the experience they needed to drop the nuclear bomb. In the end, the Enola Gay was selected as the aircraft that was to drop the bomb. In November 1945, the Straight Flush and its crew were flown back to the Roswell Army Air Field, New Mexico.

When Gil was interviewed on August 3, 1995 for a local paper on the 50th anniversary, he said was amazed at the interest people took in this event. The crew had no idea of the damage that the bomb would do when it was dropped. He said the mushroom cloud could be seen from 400 miles away. He indicated what they did save thousands of American soldier's lives. There were estimates that as many as 500,000 US soldiers would be killed in an attack on Japan. He also saw it as a good thing because after that time no country has used a nuclear bomb of any kind in war or in time of troubles. He said people are talking more and discussing things now rather than fighting.

This was an interesting event in the history of the United States and one of our relatives was involved and present at the event.

James "Jim" Bernard Niceley (1938 -)

James "Jim" Bernard Niceley (Harvey Tarver Niceley -9, James Buchanan "Whistling Jim" Niceley -8, Wesley Nicely -7, William Nicely -6, Jonas "John" Kniseley Sr. -5, Michael Kniceley -4, Antonius Kristopher "Anthony" Kneussel Jr. -3, Antonius Kristopher Knussli Sr. -2, Hans Knussli -1).

Jim is the son of Harvey Tarver and Mildred Elizabeth Kelley Niceley. He is another of our family researchers and an author of a book on his family. He wrote about the adventures of his father in a book titled "A Walking Shadow". There will be more information on this book in Appendix D, including purchasing information for those who are interested. He was employed in accounting and finance during his career working for companies in Tennessee, Georgia, and Pennsylvania. He served as a treasurer for Children's Bible Mission (CBM), for the Lost Sheep Ministries, and two churches. In 1974, he and his wife lived a month in an Indian Village in Southern Mexico aiding a missionary with Wycliffe Bible translators. From 1989 through 1990, he served as an Area Auditor in an eighteen country area in eastern and southern Africa from Ethiopia to Angola. He has been a part owner of several businesses and was the CFO and a performer for the Governor's Palace Theater in Pigeon Forge in TN. He and his wife were missionaries for the Southern Baptist North American Mission Board while other travels were for the Southern Baptist International Board. He worked in Indian reservations in Wyoming and South Dakota and with displaced Jews in Kiev, Ukraine to Israel and as a missionary in Venezuela. Jim also served in the US Air Force from 1956 to 1967. Since 2001, he has been conducting military funerals as chaplain and Commanding Officer of the East Tennessee Veterans Honor Guard.

Another well respected member of our Knusli family.

Sen. Frank Samuel Niceley (1947 -)

Sen. Frank Samuel Niceley (James Jacob "Jake" Niceley -9, Hugh Andrew Niceley -8, Jacob James Niceley -7, John Jackson "Jonathan?" Nicely -6, Jacob "Jake" Nicely -5, John George Kniceley -4, Antonius Kristopher "Anthony" Kneussel Jr. -3, Antonius Kristopher Knussli Sr. -2, Hans Knussli -1).

Frank is the son of James Jacob "Jake' and George Lucille Davis Niceley. He served 12 years in the Tennessee House of Representatives from 1988 to 1992 as the Republican Representative for State House District 17. The district included Deane Hills, Rocky Hill, Sequoyah Hills, and South Knox County in Knox County and most of Jefferson County. He grew up in Knox County TN and is a farmer and a businessman, a graduate of Jefferson County High School and the University of Tennessee. He was elected to Tennessee State Senate in 2012, and on January 8, 2013 in Nashville, TN, he took the oath of office to represent the citizens of Senate District 8. District 8 is comprised of Claiborne, Grainger, Hancock, Hawkins, Jefferson and Union Counties. The oath was administered by Supreme Court Justice William Koch, Jr. during the legislature's three-day organizational session. On January 11, 2013 --- State Senator Frank Niceley (R-Strawberry Plains) was appointed 2nd Vice-Chairman of the Senate Transportation Committee for the 2013-2014 legislative sessions. The appointment was made by Lt. Governor Ron Ramsey as the 108th General Assembly concluded their organizational session in Nashville this week. Senator Niceley was also appointed to the Energy, Agriculture, and Natural Resources Committee. Formerly the Conservation and Environment Committee, the Energy, Agriculture, and Natural Resources Committee and will now hear all issues regarding farming following a Senate rule change adopted on Thursday. This is in addition to energy, forestry, natural resources, conservation, game, fish, mines and minerals which already fell under the scope of the committee.

He serves on the board of the East Tennessee Historical Society Frank is another noted member of the Knusli family line.

Dwayne Larry Nicely (1965 -)

Dwayne Larry Nicely (Dennis Larry Nicely -10, Lennie Knapp Nicely Jr. -9, Lenny Knapp Nicely Sr. -8, John M. Niceley -7, St. Clair "Sinclair" Niceley -6, Anthony A. Kniceley IV -5, Anthony A. Kniceley -4, Antonius Kristopher "Anthony" Kneussel Jr. -3, Antonius Kristopher Knussli Sr. -2, Hans Knussli -1).

Larry is the son of Dennis Larry and Patrica Ann Moshier Nicely. He was a researcher with the Latter Day Saints library and using Harry Loren's original research for a base, he extended the family tree to include many additional members. He concluded his work with an update in December 2001. I also added his research to my work and was able to clear up a few misconceptions about our early ancestors by using DNA testing. I have been unable to contact Dwayne to update his bio information.

He was a valuable resource for information in developing our Knusli family tree.

CHAPTER ELEVEN

Family Information & Stories From The George H. Kneisley Line

John Kneisly (1792 – 1868)

John Kneisly (George Kneisly -4, George H. Kneisley -3, Antonius Kristopher Knussli Sr. -2, Hans Knussli -1).

John was one of the early pioneers in Ohio. He located a piece of land in the 1820's that was about 45 miles north of what would become Cincinnati, Ohio and about 8 miles east of Dayton, OH. He owned over 1,200 areas of land in the very fertile valley in that area. He was a farmer, improved his land, and farmed it for many years. A stagecoach line ran across his property for many years and a stagecoach depot had been established on the Mad River, named "Kneisly's Station". In 1855, the Dayton, Springfield, and Urbana Railroad traveled along that same basic route and the train stop on the Mad River was named Kneisly Station. Later on W. A. Simms bought the property from John and named the Kneisly station the Simms Station that was located on the Mad River and Lake Erie Railroad and the new station was named Simms Station on the interurban Dayton, Springfield, and Urbana Railway. Then along came the Wright Brothers after a successful flight in NC, they asked Simms for permission to use one of his large fields to fly their flights as they worked to improve their planes. They placed rails in the field they could use for the takeoff platform for their planes. These tracks were in a field that was named Hoffman Prairie and was close enough that people passing by in trains occasionally would see one of the Wright brothers flying a plane over the field. In 1913, a major flood in the area forced the railroad to relocate and years later, the land was purchased by the government and became the "Wight-Patterson Air Force Base" that is still on that site. If you visit there today, the rails used by the Wright Brothers are still there and if you go, you will be standing on property that was settled originally by one of your relatives, John Kneisly.

He was another early pioneer of the Knusli family.

George G. Kneisly (1812 – 1882)

George G. Kneisly (Abraham Kneisly -5, George Kneisly -4, George H. Kneisley -3, Antonius Kristopher Knussli Sr. -2, Hans Knussli -1).

George was killed under somewhat tragic and confusing circumstances. He had been living and working in Ohio for a while and had recently moved back to Rohrerstown, PA and was killed in a hotel in East Petersburg, PA. There were two different stories told of the event. One story was that he was in a sheriff's posse searching for an outlaw who was chased to the second story of an abandoned hotel. As they ascended the stairs, with George leading the way, the outlaw struck him on the head with an axe.

The other version told was that George was in a hotel, and since it was crowded, he had to sleep with a stranger. When he crawled into bed, the stranger had an axe in bed with him. George got up and reported it to the manager. Several men went with George back to the bedroom with George leading the way and when they reached the top of the stairs, the stranger killed him with the axe.

We will probably never know the true story but in either case, it was a tragic ending to George's life.

Benjamin Franklin Kneisly (1828 – 1867)

Benjamin Franklin Kneisly (John Kneisly -5, George Kneisly -4, George H. Kneisley -3, Antonius Kristopher Knussli Sr. -2, Hans Knussli -1).

Benjamin was the son of John Kneisly of Kneisly Station reported in the section above. There is not a lot of information on him but he served in the military. He was commissioned a Captain in the State Militia by Governor Todd of Ohio. He was later transferred to Federal Service and sent to Galveston TX to serve in the Quartermasters Department. He died in Military service during the worst disaster in Texas history. The Yellow fever struck very hard in the Galveston area where he was serving. It struck whole families and although no records were kept, an unofficial count was over 3,000 people died during 1867. It was spread by mosquitos and people were not aware of the cause. The first symptoms were a fever with head and body aches, dizziness and nausea. Several days later, they would feel better but the disease was destroying their liver and kidneys. Eventually their skin would turn yellow and they would slowly slip into a comma and die. Benjamin died of yellow fever on August 5, 1867 and his body was interred in a cemetery in Galveston, TX. His commission, sword, and Masonic apron were in the possession of his son John Adams Kneisley at the time of Harry Loren Kneisly's study that was competed in 1932.

Benjamin was another of our Military Veterans and was likely in the Civil War in his time in Texas.

Harry Loren Kneisly (1888 – after 1934)

Harry Loren Kneisly (Dr. Daniel H. Kneisly -7, Daniel Kneisly -6, John Kneisly -5, John Kneisly Sr. -4, George H. Kneisley -3, Antonius Kristopher Knussli Sr. -2, Hans Knussli -1).

Harry was the son of Dr. Daniel H. and Mary Eliza Mitchell Kneisly. He is most likely the first researcher of our family line in America. Most of his work centered on the three male family descendants members of Antonius Kristopher and Magdalena Hempstead Knussli Sr. line. Harry in the years from 1912 to 1932 was working with some very limited access to the files and information compared with what is available to us today on computer, internet and libraries. He found old deeds, wills, and recorded the information he found. He then worked mainly tracing family member by last names, traveling in his car to visit with the family members to request and record the information he was able to find. Once he located a relative, he obtained information on the location of the relatives they knew and then tracked them down. Once he had compiled the information he published a book titled the "Kneisly Genealogy Family History" that was copyrighted in 1932 that was based on data he compiled over 20 years. His report included the names of 685 descendants and relatives of these earliest residents in America of whom records have been obtained, and references to 150 others that were related. The following is the information he recorded under his own name in the book.

Harry was raised in Troy, OH, by his Uncle W. A. Evans, from age 6. He graduated from Ohio State University in 1911 with a degree of Mechanical Engineer in Electrical Engineering. He was experienced in all departments of engineering connected with public utility companies while with Stone and Webster, Galveston, Texas, where he was employed in 1911: With Electric Bond and Share, Dallas, TX, in 1913; he was a First Lieutenant in the Army Signal Corps in 1917-1919, during most of the that time in France in WWI; American Light and Traction, St. Paul, Minn., in 1922; Associated Gas and Electric Co., Oneonta, NY., New York City, and in Reading, PA in 1924-1932

Without his early research most of what we know about the family history would have went unrecorded and perhaps lost forever. All of our family members owe him a debt of gratitude for a job well done. He was truly the major contributor to our family history.

CHAPTER TWELVE

Family Information & Stories From The Adam Nicely Line

Anthony Nicely Sr. (1758 – 1845)
Adam Nicely Jr. (1764 – 1838)

These 2 family members were brothers and had the same ancestor line.

Anthony Nicely Sr. and Adam Nicely Jr. (Adam Nicely Sr. -3, Antonius Kristopher Knussli Sr. -2, Hans Knussli -1).

Anthony Sr. Was born in Lancaster County, PA and Adam Jr. was born near the town of Ligonier, PA. They were the sons of Adam and Elizabeth Eichart Nicely Sr. and each were willed ½ of the land or 600 acres of the 1,200 acres granted to Adam Sr. when he died. These 2 descendants were the individuals who proceeded to clear the majority of the land and began a major farming operation on the sections they owned. The Westmoreland County History book indicates that the Nicely family was responsible for spreading the excellent farming methods that spread across the valley. Both brothers were members of the Whig (Republican) political organization and were said to have never missed an election. They were both members of the Lutheran Church as indicated by the birth and marriage records of their families. They were among the first early pioneer farmers of the Ligonier Valley area in Southwestern PA. Anthony constructed a home in 1810 that is still standing and is under renovation at the current time. Anthony also constructed a barn near the house that burned to the ground in the 1890's. A new barn was reconstructed on the original site and has been maintained and reconditioned over the years and is still in good condition. Adam built a log home in 1800 that was added to and expanded several times over the years and is now inside the walls of the home that is standing on the original site. The barn

Adam built is still standing and has had renovation work on it over the years.

It is said that we inherit some of our traits and abilities through our DNA from our ancestors. Since our family was part of the group that started farming about 10,000 years ago, I suspect the farming skills of Anthony and Adam were most likely inherited by DNA.

Jacob "Crow or Tsu-Ka-We" Nicely (1770 – 1833)

Jacob "Crow or Tsu-Ka-We" Nicely (Adam Nicely Sr. -3, Antonius Kristopher Knussli Sr. -2, Hans Knussli -1).

Jacob was the 3rd son of Adam and Elizabeth Eichart Nicely Sr. and a brother to Antony Sr. and Adam Jr. and was born near the town of Ligonier, PA in 1770. He was one of the children captured in Ligonier area during the Revolutionary War. In 1775, Jacob was out with the other children picking berries on their father's farm and made several trips from the field back to the house for food and water. During one trip, several Indians came out of the woods, took Jacob, and disappeared into the woods. The other children saw him being taken and alerted their father. The Indians fled the area with Jacob, and his family summoned some of the neighbors and they proceeded to follow them. They followed them until they reached a Wilderness area where it was no longer save to follow. He was lost to the family until 1825 when a trader, visiting an Oho Seneca village saw a white man dressed as a Seneca Indian. The trader thought he resembled the Nicely family and came back to Ligonier and told Jacob's parents. A brother made the trip to the village and it turned out to be Jacob. He did not return with his brother, but said he would someday come to visit his parents, but he never did come back to Ligonier. The story of Jacob's capture became a legend in Ligonier and for 240 years, no one ever knew what happened to Jacob. In 2001, his Native American descendants went searching for his ancestors and eventually found Ron Nicely. This resulted in a reunion of the two family lines and Ron wrote a book on the story. The book titled "The Indian Capture of Jacob (Kneisle) Nicely" is available for purchase if you wish to read the rest of the story. Purchase information for this book is in Appendix D.

Matthew Gelvin Burkholder Sr. (1832 – 1909)

Matthew Gelvin Burkholder, husband of Sarah Ann "Sadie" Nicely Burkholder Sr. (George Nicely -5, Anthony Nicely Sr. -4, Adam Nicely Sr. -3, Antonius Kristopher Knussli Sr. -2, Hans Knussli -1).

Matthews's story is included here since his story was part of our history as the husband of a descendant. In addition to being married to a Nicely descendant his Burkholder ancestor was on the same ship from England that carried the Knusli family to America.

The real story of Matthew occurred during the Civil War. The company he joined was Company G of the 82nd Ohio Volunteer Infantry. His Company ended up under the command of General William Tecumseh Sherman and he was in the Union Army on the march to the sea through Atlanta, GA.

After his return to life after the Civil War, he became a well-respected writer for a newspaper in Greensburg, PA and it was said he welded a trenchant pen and his articles on the current topics of the day were both interesting and instructive. He was also made a Colonel in the local Militia in Westmoreland County. He and Sadie are buried in the Keltz Cemetery in Darlington, a small town near Ligonier.

Josiah G. "Joseph" Nicely (1849 – 1891)
David Curtin Nicely (1864 – 1891)

These 2 family members were brothers and had the same ancestor line.

Josiah and David Nicely (Anthony A. Nicely -5, Adam Nicely Jr. -4, Adam Nicely Sr. -3, Antonius Kristopher Knussli Sr. -2, Hans Knussli -1).

Josiah and David were sons of Anthony A. and Elizabeth James Nicely. Their story became known throughout many states and was written in many major papers in the US during the year of 1891. They were arrested and tried for theft and murder of an individual in Jennerstown, PA. Their story drew famous politicians and lawyers to the trial to defend or prosecute the brothers during the trial. They were convicted and sentenced to be hung in Somerset, PA and they were the first double indoor hanging in the state of PA. There were many rumors connected with the trial and the two men were the subject of many side stories during their incarnation. One of the most prominent rumors concerned their mother's family. Their mother's maiden name was Elizabeth James and it was rumored she was related to the family of Jesse James the outlaw from Missouri. The rumor which was never proven to this day was that Josiah, when he was a young man went to Missouri to visit his relatives and rode with Jesse on some of his robberies. The facts told in court by his father, indicated Josiah was at dinner with his parents at the time of the murder, which was about a 12 mile walk up over the mountain (about a 4 hour walk) in the snow from his father's home. Since the murder occurred at the time he with his parents, he could not have been at the scene of the robbery and murder. David on the other hand was at the scene but swore on the Bible before hanging that he was not the one who shot the victim. There was a lot of circumstantial evidence that led to their conviction. There were many newspaper articles and 2 books have been written about the story. The most recent book concludes that Josiah was innocent and that David was guilty. David never spoke up to defend his brother and it was believed David was part of a ring of thieves who apparently threatened to kill his wife and kids if he told who they were. So he remained silent and Josiah kept quiet for the same reason. Josiah had figured all along that when his parents testified that he was with them, he would be set free. The rumor about his Jesse James adventure was the fatal information that got him hung.

If you would like to read the whole story, the book is titled "Legends from the Frosty Sons of Thunder" by William Trall Doncaster, Jr. is available for purchase from the publisher. The purchase information is included in Appendix D in the back of this book.

This was a different time in history when justice was swift and final but not always correct. This is probably the most notorious event in our family history, sad but true.

Frederick Rankin Nicely Sr. (1887 – 1979)

Frederick Rankin Nicely Sr. (Anthony Wayne "Toby" Nicely -6, George Nicely -5, Anthony Nicely Sr. -4, Adam Nicely Sr. -3, Antonius Kristopher Knussli Sr. -2, Hans Knussli -1).

Frederick was the son of Anthony Wayne "Toby" and Amanda M. Karns Nicely. Fredrick was a self-made man. Upon graduation from 8th grade, he set tenpins at a local bowling alley in a hotel and delivered telegrams on a bicycle from Ligonier to Laughlintown (about 3 miles). He moved to Wilkinsburg, PA at age 14 and lived with his sister. He became an apprentice butcher and after 2 or 3 years at about age 16 he became the butcher at a company store in Madison, PA. After his marriage in 1909, he started working as a buyer for the Jamison Coal & Coke company store. Shortly after that, his brother Harry Nicely opened a store in Greensburg, PA and they shared working hours. Fred then took a job as the store manager at the Thompson No. 2 Mine. He then got a job at the Jeanette Tire Company on the assembly line but he left because they complained that he worked too fast and he did not want to slow down. He worked for Wilson Meats for a number of years as a butcher. Then he moved back to Ligonier, PA, bought a grocery store, and commuted from Greensburg. The commute became a problem so he sold the store and bought one in Derry, PA and was able to move into an apartment 2 houses away. He did well at this business and made a nice profit that allowed him to purchase an Indiana, PA meat packing plant and named it Nicely's Beef and Provision in 1926. He lost heavily in the stock market crash of 1929. He lost the meat packing plant during the Great Depression and bought a 62 acre fruit-orchard farm near New Oxford, PA. The farm did not work out well due to bad winter weather and he moved back to Indiana PA and set up a combination grocery/meat market. He owned this store for a number of years and then purchased Robindale Supply Company which was the store for the Penelec Power Company near Seward, PA. This store was successful and he stayed there until retirement when he was 70 years old.

Frederick was an example of the Knusli determination I see in many of our family members to advance and succeed in life despite many setbacks along the way.

Dr. Robert Frances Nicely Sr. (1912 – 1990)

Dr. Robert Frances Nicely Sr. (James Lawrence Nicely -7, Daniel James Nicely -6, Anthony A. Nicely -5, Adam Nicely Jr. -4, Adam Nicely Sr. -3, Antonius Kristopher Knussli Sr. -2, Hans Knussli -1).

Robert was the son of James Lawrence and Cordelia Piper Nicely. He was an educator in the Greensburg, PA school system for many years and was a strong influence on education in the school system. He was later named to the position of Superintendent of the Greensburg Salem School District. When the new Elementary school was built, he was honored by the School Board by naming the school the Robert F. Nicely Elementary School. He was also influential in the selection of a site for the Greensburg, PA campus of the University of Pittsburgh. This is where I attended school for most of my University classes from 1968 through 1975. They also named the street in front of his home as Nicely Place in Greensburg, PA.

He was a well-respected and influential teacher and educator in our Knusli family line.

Dr. William W. McKenna (1923 – 2001)

Dr. William W. McKenna (Edna Romayne Nicely McKenna -8, Cordelia "Dilla" Piper Nicely -7, Amanda Melisa Nicely Piper -6, George Nicely -5, Anthony Nicely Sr. -4, Adam Nicely Sr. -3, Antonius Kristopher Knussli Sr. -2, Hans Knussli -1).

William was the son of Irwin W. and Edna Romayne Nicely McKenna. He was a retired Colonel of the U.S, Air Force and joined the service after graduating Tau Beta Pi from the first Aeronautical Engineering class from Penn State University in 1943. He flew B-29 bombers in combat missions in the Korea War. He later received two graduate degrees from MIT and his doctorate in aeronautical and astronautical engineering from Ohio State University. He was director and consultant for many aerospace programs conceived in the 1960's and developed through the 1980's. He was awarded the Legion of Merit upon retirement from the U.S.A.F. in 1969. For 5 years, he was the Academic Dean at New England Aeronautical Institute (Now Daniel Webster College) and was named an Outstanding Educator in America.

A well respected soldier and educator of the Knusli family line.

William Edward Nicely (1932 - 2012)

William Edward Nicely (Ralph Elder Nicely -8, Charles Edward Nicely -7, George Allen Brown Nicely -6, George Nicely -5, Anthony Nicely Sr. -4, Adam Nicely Sr. -3, Antonius Kristopher Knussli Sr. -2, Hans Knussli -1).

William is the son of Ralph Elder and Garnet L. Mimna Nicely. He and his brother Denny had an adventure when Bill was 13 years old and Denny was 10 years old. His father had been in WWII and upon his return, he moved to CA to look for a job and a home for him and his 2nd wife. Bill and Denny were left with their mother's parents. After their father found a home and a job, he sent for Bill and Denny. He paid for bus tickets for both of them and the boys were taken to Pittsburgh, PA to catch the bus. Unfortunately, they were not given enough money to buy meals and drink for the entire trip. Through the good graces or some of the other bus riders, they helped them with food and drink. It took about 6 days to make the trip and they arrived safely. It was a very scary event for both of them, sleeping on the bus and in bus stations.

Bill's life took an unusual turn when he was 16. He decided it was time for him to get a part-time job and he set out walking to a business area to try and find work. As he was crossing the railroad tracks between two buildings, he ran into the owner of the company that was using the 2 buildings. The owner's name was John Renaker, and he asked Bill what he was doing between the 2 buildings. Bill explained he was off high school for the Easter Holiday and was seeking a job. John asked him to come into his building so he could show him what they were making and to see if perhaps he could find a job for him. John hired Bill as a part-time employee on that day in 1948 to do odd jobs. After Bill graduated from high school he continued to work for the company and became a full-time employee. Bill stayed with the company until he died in 2012. He became John's right hand man and helped to design and to manufacture the molds used to make the well-known Hagen-Renaker Inc. ceramic animal figurines. These figurines are now American made collectables that are still being produced today and you will find them in many gift shops. Bill served in many different positions including General Manager and in later years, as the institutional memory of the company and was active in the company for 64 years right up until his death at 80 years of age.

The sadness in his life was that his mother left him and Denny with her parents while their father was in World War II and he never saw her again. Bill's life is a remarkable story of determination that seems to be in many of the Knusli descendants, by making the best of our situations.

Ronald Earl Nicely (1937 -)

Ronald Earl Nicely (Robert Earl Nicely -8, Charles Edward Nicely -7, George Allen Brown Nicely -6, George Nicely -5, Anthony Nicely Sr. -4, Adam Nicely Sr. -3, Antonius Kristopher Knussli Sr. -2, Hans Knussli -1).

Ronald is the son of Robert Earl "Cappy" and Florence Rose McDowell Nicely and the author of the book you are reading. He was born in his Grandfather farmhouse on Nicely Road in Ligonier, PA. He spent the first 23 years of his life living in the small town of Ligonier and worked at many different jobs during those years: farm work for his grandparents, paperboy, store clerk, gas station attendant, used and new car polish boy, farm equipment mechanic, used car renewal and parts assistant, and service station manager. At age 23, he was drafted into the U. S. Army for 2 years and was trained in radio repair and worked on aircraft radios and communications equipment. When he was released from active duty, he joined the Ligonier National Guard and served an additional 4 years. He was hired by Kennametal Inc. in Latrobe, PA, shortly after he returned from active duty and began a 34 year career with them. He worked in many different positions: Research Clerk. Sales Correspondent, Pricing Estimator, Supervisor of Specialty Pricing, Marketing Research, and for the last 25 years, he held the position of Business Forecaster, with responsibility for sales and production forecasts worldwide. In 1968 through 1975, he attended evening school at the University of Pittsburgh at Greensburg in PA and obtained a BS Degree in Business Administration.

After his retirement from Kennametal, he started a Forecast Consulting business for the Metalworking Industry and still is consulting at the current time. In 1998, he began working on his family genealogy that resulted in testing of his DNA and serving as Coordinator of the Nicely Surname on the Family Tree DNA website and writing two books on his family. He continues to do research on the family line and has connected with many relatives who are searching for more information on their family line.

He is an active Participant in promoting and advancing the history of the Knusli Family.

John Robert "Jack" Nicely (1938 -)

John Robert "Jack" Nicely (John Emerson Nicely -8, Rev. Emerson Lorenzo Nicely -7, Josiah G. "Joseph" Nicely -6, Anthony A. Nicely -5, Adam Nicely Jr. -4, Adam Nicely Sr. -3, Antonius Kristopher Knussli Sr. -2, Hans Knussli -1).

John is the son of John Emerson and Martha Roberts Lochrie Nicely and is another of our family genealogists. He is a Great Grandson of Josiah Nicely and supplied a lot of information to my research and to the researcher who wrote the book on the Nicely brothers history. He was one of the first members of Adam Nicely Jr.'s line to get in touch with me and gave me his family information that allowed me to begin expanding our family information. He and I worked together and finally determined it was Adam Nicely Sr., who was the first family member to move to Ligonier. He was also instrumental in finding the disposition of Antonius Kristopher Knussli's will in Lancaster, PA. We also worked at the Mennonite Historical Society to gather information on the location of the property Antonius was granted. He was very helpful in support of the research of the family. I would not have been able to expand my research without his help and assistance.

He is a noted example of the dedication to the research, reporting, recording, and extending of our family history.

Dr. Robert Frances Nicely Jr. (1940 -)

Dr. Robert Francis Nicely Jr. (Dr. Robert Frances Nicely Sr. -8, James Lawrence Nicely -7, Daniel James Nicely -6, Anthony A. Nicely -5, Adam Nicely Jr. -4, Adam Nicely Sr. -3, Antonius Kristopher Knussli Sr. -2, Hans Knussli -1).

Robert is the son of Robert Francis and Jean Isabelle Baird Nicely Sr. who is listed above. He followed in his father's footsteps in becoming an educator. He is listed in the Who's Who of America. He is currently a professor of education and the coordinator of continuing education and commonwealth relations at Penn State University.

He is another of our noted educators in the Knusli family line.

Don Arthur Gilmore (1953 -)

Don Arthur Gilmore (Joan Louise Armel Gilmore -9, Ethel E. Leonard Armel -8, Hannah Burkholder Leonard -7, Sarah Ann "Sadie" Nicely Burkholder -6, George Nicely -5, Anthony Nicely Sr. -4, Adam Nicely Sr. -3, Antonius Kristopher Knussli Sr. -2, Hans Knussli -1).

Don is the son of Edward J. and Joan Louise Armel Gilmore. Don is the President for Dakota Engineering Associates Inc. in Etna, PA. He has been the individual who was instrumental in the renovation and repair of the Keltz Cemetery in Darlington, PA. It is the burial site for the earliest member of our Ligonier branch of the Knusli family. It was abandoned many years ago, then the Riggs family maintained it for many years and then it was turned over to the Ligonier Historical Society who arranged for mowing and general cleanup 3 times a year. In 2004, Don found me and we started working on improving the area. The headstones were cleaned and a large number had fallen or were ready to fall. Don brought some friends with him, and some of the Ligonier relatives joined in and many improvements were made and several new headstones were installed. Don is working towards setting up a trust so that funds will be available to keep it maintained into the future. This cemetery while small contains around 130 graves, many without markers, with a large majority of the headstones are markers for relatives of the Nicely family.

Don is also the builder and owner of a Bonneville automobile that he ran last year for the first time. His fastest run last year was around 200 MPH. He is working to improve the speed on his 2014 run this summer.

Don has invested time effort and money to help preserve the history of our family.

Todd Garrett Pelkey (1967 -)

Todd Garrett Pelkey (Donna Gene Stoner Pelkey -9, Dorothy Marie Nicely Stoner -8, George B. "Bert" Nicely -7, Ezra G. Nicely -6, Anthony A. Nicely -5, Adam Nicely Jr. -4, Adam Nicely Sr. -3, Antonius Kristopher Knussli Sr. -2, Hans Knussli -1).

Todd is the son of Lewis Eugene and Donna Gene Stoner Pelkey. Todd is also another one of our family researcher and was inspired by his Grandmother to pursue the family tree and history. He gave me all of the Ligonier Nicely family tree information he had gathered to aid me in putting together a nearly complete tree that has been added to my file. He also maintained a web site with all his family history for a number of years.

Adam Brett Nicely (1981 -)

Adam Brett Nicely (Edward Joseph Nicely -10, William Frederick Nicely -9, William Houseberg Nicely -8, Ezra Gelvin Nicely -7, John Harnett "Drover" Nicely -6, Anthony Wayne Nicely -5, Anthony Nicely Sr. -4, Adam Nicely Sr. -3, Antonius Kristopher Knussli Sr. -2, Hans Knussli -1).

Adam is the son of Edward Joseph and Delores Epps Nicely. Adam was named after his 6th Great Grandfather Adam Nicely, who was the first of our family line to move to Ligonier PA and who served in the Revolutionary War as a Frontier Ranger. He is currently the Co-Producer of the Saturday Night Live show on NBC. He earned a BA in Communication studies at the University of North Carolina. While in his junior year, he moved to New York to accept a job editing for SNL, and completed his degree by online classes and wrote a term paper about SNL. He became involved with broadcast technology and was instrumental in the transition from analog to digital acquisition and post production. He was recognized for his contribution to NBC Universal's Emmy Award at the 2011 Technology and Engineering Emmy Awards. In 2008 he assisted with the technology and staffing to launch Late Night with Jimmy Fallon which later became The Tonight Show with Jimmy Fallon and is credited as a Technical Consultant.

He is a very knowledgeable and well known descendant of the Knusli family.

Summary

I started to write this page as a conclusion but in retrospect, this is more of a beginning of the rest of our family history. In spite of where we have been, where we are headed is a mystery. So I thought it might be more appropriate to try and summarize our history and what I have seen, heard, and found.

In spite of the difficulties our family has experienced there seems to be an undying spirit to move us into the future. We strived to find a place where we could enjoy God's blessings and enjoy the freedoms he offered to us. The persecution our ancestors suffered only seemed to strengthen them as they moved through the last 50,000 plus years. They used their strength of character and their faith and belief in God to continue to live and prosper. This strength helped to push them forward to the unknowing future. In the past when we failed, we did not quit but continued to move forward. Looking back is also a trait in our family. Many people have recorded the history to pass to the future. It is said if you know the past, you are less likely to repeat the failures of the past. Also knowing the past helps us with the problems we face in current day life.

There is an amazing likeness in attitude, features and characteristics of many of our family members. Also, many of our family members have special skills that seem to crop up in some but not in all. One of these areas is in musical talents. Some of our family members are very skilled musicians. If you search on the internet, you can find quite a few who are making or trying to make their living doing so. I personally know of 3 family members who have the unusual skill of being able to pick up a stringed instrument and begin to play without the ability to read the music and I am sure there could be many others with the same skill. They are able to play by ear. There are many skilled carpenters, machine operators, mechanics of all kinds, professionals in all different specialties and most have made their living at these trades. Intelligent also is evident in many who have used their intelligence in different positions to benefit mankind in medicine and in educational areas.

The Journey of our family will hopefully continue for many years and there will be many new stories of joy, hardships, and struggles, and with God's blessings, we will continue to have an influence on our own future and live our lives to the fullest of our God given abilities and talents.

It is my hope that someone will pick up the torch and keep the fire of our history burning into the future.

It has been a labor of love of family to put this together and define our past. I was able to go farther beyond my original expectations in finding my ancestors and what they did and who they were. I hope you find some comfort in knowing more about our family.

Appendix A

Since our family was living in the Bible lands during the time of the Bible, I am including a listing of Jesus's ancestors as printed in the Bible. It's possible that we may have been a descendant of one of these individuals or at the very least, we would have been a cousin to the members of this family line. As I mentioned earlier there have been Y-DNA tests with Hebrew descendants who had the Cohan Marker in their Y-DNA and it was proved that they were very distant cousins.

Jesus's Ancestor Listing

Taken from Matthew 1:1-16 (New International Version)

The Genealogy of Jesus

1 A record of the genealogy of Jesus Christ the son of David, the son of Abraham:
2 Abraham was the father of Isaac,
Isaac the father of Jacob,
Jacob the father of Judah and his brothers,
3 Judah the father of Perez and Zerah, whose mother was Tamar,
Perez the father of Hezron,
Hezron the father of Ram,
4 Ram the father of Amminadab,
Amminadab the father of Nahshon,
Nahshon the father of Salmon,
5 Salmon the father of Boaz, whose mother was Rahab,
Boaz the father of Obed, whose mother was Ruth,
Obed the father of Jesse,
6 and Jesse the father of King David.
David was the father of Solomon, whose mother had been Uriah's wife,

7 Solomon the father of Rehoboam,
   Rehoboam the father of Abijah,
   Abijah the father of Asa,
8 Asa the father of Jehoshaphat,
   Jehoshaphat the father of Jehoram,
   Jehoram the father of Uzziah,
9 Uzziah the father of Jotham,
   Jotham the father of Ahaz,
   Ahaz the father of Hezekiah,
10 Hezekiah the father of Manasseh,
   Manasseh the father of Amon,
   Amon the father of Josiah,
11 and Josiah the father of Jeconiah and his brothers at the time of the exile to Babylon.
12 After the exile to Babylon:
   Jeconiah was the father of Shealtiel,
   Shealtiel the father of Zerubbabel,
13 Zerubbabel the father of Abiud,
   Abiud the father of Eliakim,
   Eliakim the father of Azor,
14 Azor the father of Zadok,
   Zadok the father of Akim,
   Akim the father of Eliud,
15 Eliud the father of Eleazar,
   Eleazar the father of Matthan,
   Matthan the father of Jacob,
16 and Jacob the father of Joseph, the husband of Mary, of whom was born Jesus, who is called Christ.

Appendix B

Since our family line was part of the Middle East at the time of Abraham's descendants, I thought it would be of interest to show the kinds of food that were consumed by our ancestors during that period of time. A catering service, Myrians Table presents a four course meal from the "Land of Milk and Honey" in the area where the author lives. This is their menu for the dinner. I attended this dinner on two occasions and loved the food and preparation.

Middle Eastern Dinner

Featuring Foods of the Bible

Mazza Platter with
Hummus, Feta Cheese, Cucumbers,
Olives, Eggplant Dip, Cucumber with Yogurt Sauce
Tomatoes, and Flat Bread

Lentils, Rice, Caramelized Onions, and Zucchini

Barley with Chicken, Carrots, and Onions

Kibbee and Tabouli
Beans with Lamb in a Tomato Sauce over Rice

Baklava, Almond Cookies, Pomegranate, Dates, Figs, and Grapes

Appendix C

Our Family Veterans

The following list is based on the information that I have gathered and is not an entire list of all Veterans. If anyone or knows of a relative, who was a veteran and not on the list, let me know I will add their name and in the event there happens to be a revision of the book. I will add them to my list and include them in any revision.

Email me at nicelyguy@msn.com

Revolutionary War Veterans.

Ambrose, John Frederick (1737-1821). He served as a 1st Lt. in Captain Henry Rhoads Company, Bedford County, enlisted on Dec, 10, 1777.

Eager, George (1737-1819) He served as a Captain in the Frontier Rangers in the Ligonier Valley, PA area in the Revolutionary War. He is buried in Keltz Cemetery.

Keltz Jr., George Adam (1758-1837) He served as a Private in the Frontier Rangers near Ligonier, PA. (Also served in the War of 1812)

Keltz Sr., George Adam (1734-1784) He served as a Frontier Ranger under Captain Richard Williams near Ligonier PA.

Kneisly, Christian (1757-1836) He served as a Private 2nd class in Captain Duncan's Company, 6th Battalion, Lancaster County Militia, in the Revolutionary War. His name appears on the Honor Roll, Memorial Bell Tower, at Valley Forge.

Kneisly, Christian (1757-1836). He served in the Revolutionary War along with his brother Michael.

Kneisly, Michael (1751-1793). He served in the Revolutionary War in a Company from Little Britain Township, Lancaster PA.

Kniseley Sr., Jacob (1741-1830). He served as a Sargent in Captain Jonathan Clark's Company, of the 8th Virginia Regiment on foot, commanded by Col. Abraham Bowman in the Revolutionary War.

Knisely Sr., John (1752-1834). He was a Private in the Revolutionary War, and later the founder of New Philadelphia, OH.

Nicely Sr., Adam (1730-1826). He served in the Revolutionary War as a Frontier Ranger in the 8th Regiment in Ligonier, PA area as a Private and served under Captain Richard Williams. He also served as a wagoner in 1758 to 1761, carrying goods to the British soldiers stationed at Fort Ligonier during the French and Indian War.

War of 1812 Veterans

Keltz Jr., George Adam (1758-1837) He served in the War of 1812 as a Lieutenant. (Also served in the Revolutionary War)

Kniceley Sr., Jonas "John" (1769-1817). He was a volunteer in the 4th (Boyd's) Virginia Militia in the War of 1812.

Kniseley, Samuel A. (1784-1867). He enlisted for service in the War of 1812 and assisted in the construction of the blockhouse at Mansfield, OH. He was a 1st Lieutenant in his company and was noted as a brave and daring soldier.

Civil War Veterans

Ambrose, John (1837 -1898) He was shot through the neck at Bull Run and shot in the right knee at Gettysburg.

Aukerman, Anthony (1933-bef. 1922). He served in the Civil War.

Burkholder Sr., Matthew Gelvin (1832-1909) He served in the Civil War and was with General Sherman on the March to the Sea.

Fry, Michael (ca 1828-1902) His tombstone shows he served in Company C. 84th Regiment of the PA Volunteers in the Civil War.

Hougendobler, Amos R. (1843-1919). He served in Company K. 5th Regiment of PRVC in the Civil Was.

Keltz, Anthony (1836-1890) He served in the Civil War.

Kneisly, Abraham (1842-1919) He was a 90 day man in the Civil War.

Kniceley, John Samuel (1807-1891) He served in the Union Army in Company F. 10th West Virginia Volunteer infantry in the Civil War.

Knicely, Ebenezer (1812 or 1822-bef. 1912) He served with Company E. of the 58th Virginia Militia as a Private in the Civil War.

Knisely, George Washington (1842-1931). He served in the Civil War.

Knisley, John B. (1838-1904). He served in Company A, 21st Regiment in the PA Calvary in the Civil War.

Knisley, Richard (1829-bef. 1919). He served in Company A, 175th Infantry in the Civil War.

McDowell, Hiram Y. (1844-1930). He served in Company C., 211th Regiment of the Pennsylvania Volunteers in the Civil War.

McDowell, Israel (1840-ca 1864). He was killed in the Civil War.

Muck, John J. (1832-1905). He served in the Civil War.

Niceley, John Alexander (1824-1911) He enlisted in the Confederate Army in 1862 and served until Lee's Surrender. He was in the battles of Droop Mountain, Lynchburg, Cedar Creek, Snickers Gap and Gordonsville. He served in the 25th Virginia Infantry and the 9th Battalion Virginia Infantry.

Nicely, Adam (1833-1873). He served in the Civil War.

Nicely, Anderson (1815-ca1863). He enlisted in the Confederate Army in 1862 in the 8th TN Cavalry Brigade, Brigadier General Charles Clark's battalion of the Central Army of Kentucky. He fought in the 1862 battle at Fort Donaldson near Dover, TN and the battle of Clarksville, TN. He died in a West Tennessee Civil War battle.

Nicely, Asa McClelland (1857-1864). He died in Salisbury prison in NC during the Civil War.

Nicely, Asher K. (1839-1898). He enlisted in 1861 in Company G. 135th Regiment of the PA Volunteers and served nine months. In February 1864, he re-enlisted in Company G, 1st Regiment, PA Volunteers and served a total of 3 years during the Civil war.

Nicely, Dudley (1827-bef. 1917). He served during the Civil War.

Nicely, Fuller John (1837-1913). He served during the Civil War.

Nicely, Isaac C. (1843-1863) He was a Private in Company G. 135th Regiment of the PA Volunteers in the Civil War and died in Washington DC during the War.

Nicely, Jacob C. (1844-1866). His tombstone indicates he was a veteran of the Civil War and family history indicates he died due to injuries from the war in 1866. The only record we could find was a Jacob B. Nicely that was mustered into Company A PA 1st Calvary on 7/25/1861 and mustered out 9/9/1864 at Philadelphia. We assume there was confusion of the middle initial of B versus C, which sound the same.

Nicely, Jacob James (1828-1909). He joined the 8th or 9th US Calvary during the Civil War as a Captain. He fought for the Union and spelled his name Nicely like the Confederate Nicely's in Granger County, TN. After the war he changed his name to Niceley perhaps to make both sides happy or confused.

Nicely, James A. (1819-1870). He joined the Union Army and so did his brothers. His cousin Andrew Jackson fought for the Confederacy. Nicely brothers fought Nicely cousins during the Civil War.

Noel, Jonas (1839-1928) He served two enlistments in the Civil War in Company C., 11th PA Volunteer Infantry.

Romig, Owen T. (1840-1935) He served in the Union Army as a Private in Company F. of the 161st Ohio Infantry in the Civil War.

Stein, Henry M. (1842- bef 1932) He served in Company E, 211th Regiment of the PA Volunteers.

Pancho Villa Expedition Veteran

Between the Civil War and World War 1, there was a military action by the U.S. Calvary that was the last horse mounted Campaign of the U.S. Calvary.

Pancho Villa raided Columbus, New Mexico and killed a number of Americans. President Wilson sent 5,000 men of the U.S. Army under General John Pershing into Mexico to capture Villa. They employed aircraft and trucks for the first time in US Army history. Pershing's force chased Villa until February 1917. The search for Villa was unsuccessful. However, some of Villa's senior commanders (Colonel Candelario Cervantes, General Francisco Beltran, Beltrán's son and Villa's second-in-command Julio Cardenas) and 190 of his men were killed during the expedition.

The Mexican population was against having US troops in Mexican territories. There were several demonstrations of their opposition to the Punitive Expedition and that counted towards the failure of that expedition. During the expedition, one of Villa's top generals, Pablo Lopez was captures and executed on June 13, 1916.

One of the Knusli descendants was involved in this campaign.

Whitecrow Sr., Mayo Sidney (1893-1957). He served in the 5th Calvary in the Machine Gunners Troup and was among the troops who chased Pancho into Mexico.

World War I Veterans

Armor, William. He was assumed to have been killed in WWI since he never returned home.

Burkholder, Robert E. (1925-2004) He served with the U. S. Air Force in Italy during the World War I.

Cogan, Ralph (1899-1951). He served in the U.S. Army in WWI and he died at home the result of mustard gas poisoning from the war.

Deise, Thomas Alexander (1899-2000) He served in the U.S. Navy during WWI.

Geeting, Milton E. (1882-1965). He was a Veteran of World War I.

Kneisly, Harry Loren (1888-bef. 1932) He was a 1st Lieutenant in the U.S. Army Signal Corps in France during WWI.

Knisely, Samuel Henry (1875-1951). He served in World War I.

Queer, Harry M. "Tink" (1895-1978) He served in France during World War I and volunteered for World War II but was turned down due to his age.

World War II Veterans

Aikins, William Donald (1921-1993). He served in the U.S. Army marching band in Italy during World War II.

Ambrose, Bert Eugene (1906-1994). He served in the U.S. Army during World War II.

Byers, Jacob E. (1916-2000). He served in the U.S. Army in Europe and Asia during World War II.

Coon, Harold Russell (1916-1969) He served in the U.S. Army military Signal Division in World War II.

Darr, James Russell "Trigger" (1911-1976). He served in the U.S. Army Air Force in WWII.

Demmitt, Robert Frederick (1913-1967). He served in the U.S. Army in Europe in World War II. He was in the Invasion of Normandy and was wounded. He was sent to a hospital in England for recovery. He had some difficult times but would never discuss them saying they were better off forgotten.

Ford (Good), Eugene Paul (ca 1921-ca 1945). He was a B24 Pilot in the Army Air Force in WWII and died in the service of his country.

Harr, Robert G. (1923-2009) He served in the U.S Navy during WWII.

Hunter Sr., Thomas Bailey (1923-2011) He served in the Pacific in World War II. He was one of 14 men from Ligonier PA who were on Guam Island and formed a Guam Club.

Johnson, Glenn E. (1924-2011) He was in the U.S. Navy in WWII.

Keltz, Benjamin R. "Ben" (1916-2009) He was in the U.S. Army Air Corps in WWII.

Keltz, John Jacob "Jack" (1921-2005) He served in the U.S. Army Air Corps in WWII.

Leslie Sr., John Robert "Bob" (1924-2008). He was a veteran of the U.S. Army in World War II and after the War, he became the Commander and Coordinator of the PA National Guard in Ligonier, PA for over 30 years.

Lute Sr., Charles W. (1926-2010). He served in the U.S. Army during World War II.

Lute, George William (1925-2011). He served in the U.S. Navy during World War II.

Madak, Robert (1925-2007). He served in the U.S. Navy as a radio operator in the Philippines during World War II.

McDowell, Emmett E. (1917-2009). He served in the U.S. Army as a Sergeant during World War II.

McDowell, John Austin (1924-1998). He served in the U.S. Navy during World War II.

McClain, John Clifton Hagerman "Jack" (1919-1995) He served in the U.S. Army Air Force during World War II. He was stationed in Biloxi, MS due to allergy problems. He worked on airplanes.

McKenna Dr., William W. (1923-2001). He served in the U.S. Air Force during 3 wars (World War II, Korean War, and Vietnam War) from 1943 to 1969. During the Korean War as a command pilot, he flew B-29 "Flying Fortresses" in combat missions.

Naugle, J. Clifford (1921-2003). He served in the U.S. Army during World War II and was the First Sergeant of the Ligonier, PA Army National Guard for over 20 years.

Niceley, Gillon Truett "Gil" (1923-2005). He served during World War II as the tail gunner on the B-29 "Straight Flush" that was the plane that proceeded the B-29 "Enola Gay" into Japan on the bombing of Hiroshima Japan. (His story is listed in the stories section of this book.)

Nicely, Charles George (1926-2005). He served in the U.S. Army with the 69th Infantry Division. He was awarded the Purple Heart and he participated in the Battle of the Bulge in Belgium.

Nicely, Clarence (1923-2011). He served in the U.S. Army in World War II in the Philippines and attained the rank of Sergeant.

Nicely, Glenn Calvin (1924-2006). He served in the Merchant Marines during World War II.

Nicely, Lewis Bailey (1925-2011) He served in the U.S. Navy during World War II.

Nicely, Ralph Elder (1908-1966) He served in the U.S. Army during World War II. He was in Paris, France after the Liberation of France.

Nicely, Ralph Martin (1922-2008) He served in the U>S> Army during World War II.

Nicely, Warren Lindley "Red" (1916-1973). He was in the U.S Army and served as a tank gunner during World War II.

Nicely, William Howard (1930-2008) He served in the U.S. Army in the Korean War and later in the Ligonier PA National Guard.

Norris Jr., George F. (1920-2007) He served in the U.S. Navy as a gunner's mate during World War II.

Norris, John W. (1923-2010) He served in the U.S. Army in the 29th Division during World War II.

Piper Sr., Ray Lewis "Pap" (1925-2013) He served under General George Patton in Metz, France during World War II and was wounded and sent to San Antonio, TX for recuperation.

Shadron Sr., Warren R. (1924-2007) At 18 years of age he joined the U.S. Navy during World War II. He served on three aircraft carrier during the war, most notably the USS Midway. He was an original crew member and an original plank member and owns one plank from the flight deck of that ship which is the right of original crews.

Stynchula, Frank Joseph (1925-2001) He joined the U.S Air Force during World War II and served through three wars; World War II, Korean War, and Vietnam War, before retiring. He attained the rank of Master Sergeant and most of the time was spent maintaining the golf courses and grounds at the bases where he was stationed.

Korean War Veterans

Aikins, Frederick Nelson (1941- 1975) He served in the U.S. Army in the Korean War.

Anderson, Harvey J. (1932-2010) He served in the U.S. Army.

Coon, Eugene Lewis (1929-1998) He served in the U.S. Army after WWII in 1947 and 1948 then later reenlisted in 1950 for the Korean War and served as a combat infantryman in the 1st Calvary Division.

Hutchison, Raymond Charles "Gabe" (1928-2002) He served in the U.S. Army in the Korean War.

McKenna Dr., William W. (1923-2001). He served in the U.S. Air Force during 3 wars (World War II, Korean War, and Vietnam War) from 1943 to 1969. During the Korean War as a command pilot, he flew B-29 "Flying Fortresses" in combat missions.

Nicely, Robert Allen (1932-2010) He served in the U.S. Air Force during the Korean War. He also served as the post commander of the Ligonier Legion 267, post commander of the Ligonier VFW 734, and District 27 commander of the VFW and was a member of the Ligonier Valley Veteran's Honor Guard.

Shepler, Gerald Bolby "Bud' (1933-) He served in the U.S. Army during the Korean War.

Vietnam War Veterans

Ambrose, Robert Dewey (1953-2010). He served in the U. S. Air Force during the Vietnam War.

Graham, Gregory C. (1947-2009). He was a member of Special Services in the U.S. Army and served in the Vietnam War.

McDermott, Robert (1949-). He served during the Vietnam War.

McKenna Dr., William W. (1923-2001). He served in the U.S. Air Force during 3 wars (World War II, Korean War, and Vietnam War) from 1943 to 1969. During the Korean War as a command pilot, he flew B-29 "Flying Fortresses" in combat missions.

Niceley, James "Jim" Bernard (1938-) He served in the U.S. Air Force during the Vietnam War.

Nicely, Robert Lee (1938-) He served in the Vietnam War.

Nicely, Ronald Earl (1937-) He served in the U.S. Army between the Korean and the Vietnam War. He was in the PA National Guard during the early years of the Vietnam War.

Appendix D

Following is a list of several books that are available for purchase that were written about our family or members of our family. You might want to add to your library of Knusli history.

"The Indian Capture of Jacob (Kneisle) Nicely"

Author: Ronald Earl Nicely

This is a true story of a descendant of the Adam Nicely Sr. line of Ligonier PA. Jacob Nicely was captured in 1775 at age 5 and never returned to the family. In 2003, the Native American descendants of Jacob located the Nicely family in Ligonier and a reunion was held where the 2 branches were reunited.

You can go to www.lulu.com to read more about the story. There are several options to purchase the book. Also at Lulu check the website for books http//www.lulu

For comments, questions, and autographed book purchases
Contact Ronald Earl Nicely directly at
nicelyguy@msn.com

This book can also be ordered online at
The Lulu Bookstore at
http://www.lulu.com/shop/shop.ep
or
as an eBook at one of the following
Amazon Kindle
Sony e-Reader
Barnes and Noble Nook
Kobo (Borders) e-Reader
Google eBook site.

"A Walking Shadow"

Author: James Bernard Niceley

This book covers the actual event of James's father. A single act of uncontrolled anger turned a typical East Tennessee teen into a fugitive. Running from the law, Harv Niceley embarked on what would become a ten year trek across the United States, during which he lived by his wits, his tenacity, and his own set of rules. Ultimately, his search for meaning and purpose took him back to his roots. Based upon actual people and events, from 1840 – 1930. A Walking Shadow follows the tale of both a man and a country, at war with themselves, and searching for peace with God and each other.

Unfortunately, his book is no longer in publication but when I searched the internet, there were some books available for sale used and new. So if you are interested, you should be able search the internet and find a copy to purchase.

"Legends from the Frosty Sons of Thunder"

Author William Trall Doncaster, Jr.

This book covers the story of the Nicely Brothers, Joseph and David from the Ligonier PA area. The brothers were tried for the murder of a man in Jennerstown, PA and tried in court in Somerset, PA and became the first double indoor hanging in PA. The author covers the area and events surrounding the murder and the trial and the hanging. The Old Forbes Military Road that runs through the Somerset County in PA is the source of rich American history and folklore. Since their occurrence in 1889, the controversial Nicely brothers murder trial and the devastating Johnstown flood have become two of this area's most remembered historical events. Both have been recorded through oral history and embellished, and have become enduring legends. This was in an era of storytelling, when the American wilderness was vast and rich with danger and possibility. These stories, along with many others are brought to life in this account of Pennsylvania folklore and rural life punctuated by backwoods superstitions and romantic heroes and antiheroes. Author Dr. William Doncaster (now deceased) writes

"Both became matters of national concern and interest. Both emblazoned the town in the valley and the village in the mountains with deep scars, unforgettable memories, and troubling questions that continue to keep each legend alive.

This book can be purchased at:
Brandylane Publishers, Inc.
5 South First St.
Richmond, VA 23219
Phone 804 644-3090
www.brandylanepublishers.com

Appendix E

Who's Who of America Family Members

The following people are listed in the book "Who's Who of America" that I do not have in my genealogy files. Since I do not have their family link, I cannot place them in a family line. If you find your name in the list or if anyone reading this listing finds a person, they know or are related to, please contact the author of the book to establish their link, so I can list them in the proper line if I decide to update the book. Several individuals have been listed in their line as being in Who's Who of America and are not included in this list.

Email nicelyguy@msn.com

Knisely Surname Descendant

Nathaniel Mckay Kneisly *(Deceased)*
Publishing Company Executive; Born: 1892
Country: United States

Knicely Surname Descendants

Carroll Franklin Knicely *(Deceased)*
Publishing Executive; Born: 1928
Location: Glasgow, KY
Country: United States

Doris Kohne Knicely
Secondary Educator; Born: 1942
Location: Woodstock, VA
Country: United States

Howard V. Knicely
Human Resource Executive; Born: 1936
Location: Chagrin Falls, OH
Country: United States

James Jeffrey Knicely
Lawyer; Born: 1946
Location: Williamsburg, VA
Country: United States

Nancy Carol Knicely
Psychiatric Nurse; Born: 1945
Country: United States

Kniseley Surname Descendants

Ralph Marion Kniseley
Pathologist, Nuclear Medicine Physician; Born: 1920

Richard Newman Kniseley
Consultant; Born: 1930
Location: Ames, IA
Country: United States

Knisely Surname Descendants

Beth Ann Knisely
Graphic Designer; Born: 1959
Location: Southfield, MI
Country: United States

Charles William Knisely
Engineering Educator, Researcher, Consultant; Born: 1952
Location: Lewisburg, PA
Country: United States

Debra Sue Knisely
Secondary School Educator; Born: 1952
Location: Pembroke Pines, FL
Country: United States

Douglas Charles Knisely
Accountant; Born: 1948
Location: Grove City, OH
Country: United States

Jay Wallace Knisely
Plastics Company Executive; Born: 1947
Location: Denver, CO
Country: United States

Karin Ingrid Knisely
Biologist, Educator; Born: 1958
Location: Lewisburg, PA
Country: United States

Marc O. Knisely
Lawyer; Born: 1950
Location: Austin, TX
Country: United States

Ralph Franklin Knisely
Retired Microbiologist; Born: 1927
Location: Frederick, MD
Country: United States

Sally Knisely *(Deceased)*
Psychotherapist; Born: 1917

William Hagerman Knisely *(Deceased)*
Anatomical Sciences Educator Emeritus, Retired University Dean; Born: 1922

Knisley Surname Descendants

Elsilynn Knisley
Music Educator; Born: 1957
Location: Ooltewah, TN
Country: United States

Patrick Allen Knisley
Advertising Company Executive; Born: 1949
Location: New York, NY
Country: United States

Stephen Bruce Knisley
Biomedical Engineering Educator; Born: 1951
Location: Durham, NC
Country: United States

Nicely Surname Descendants

I have to qualify this particular line since some Nicely individuals are not of the Knusli family line. There is a group in the Knusli line and a group with a different Y-DNA who are in the Nusli line and not related. Some of these individuals may or may not be in the Knusli line. If you know any of these people, please have them contact the author to clarify their family line.

Alan Ross Nicely
Secondary School Educator; Born: 1955
Location: Mableton, GA
Country: United States

Andrew Abbott Nicely
Lawyer
Location: Washington, DC
Country: United States

Constance Marie Nicely
Business Couch, Career Councilor. Born: 1955
Location: Maryland Heights, MO
Country: United States

Denise Ellen Nicely
Elementary School Educator; Born: 1966
Location: Chesapeake, VA

Donna D. Nicely
Library Director
Location: Nashville, TN
Country: United States

Harold Elliott Nicely *(Deceased)*
Clergyman; Born: 1900
Country: United States

James Mount Nicely *(Deceased)*
Association Executive; Born: 1899
Country: United States

James Richard Nicely
Insurance Company Executive; Born: 1940
Location: Oklahoma City, OK
Country: United States

Kathleen Clare Nicely
University Program Director; Born: 1970
Location: College Park, MD
Country: United States

Matthew R. Nicely
Lawyer
Location: Washington, DC
Country: United States

Olza M. (Tony) Nicely
Insurance Company Executive; Born: 1943
Location: Washington, DC
Country: United States

Philip A. Nicely
Lawyer; Born: 1942
Location: Indianapolis, IN
Country: United States

Tanna Hurd Nicely
Science Educator, Consultant; Born: 1967
Location: Blaine, TN
Country: United States

Timothy Nicely
Producer, Writer; Born: 1944
Location: Tarzana, CA
Country: United States

The variety of occupations listed above is an indication of the variety of capabilities of our family line. Since part of each person's DNA comes from 7 generations of parents and grandparents from all the different ancestor lines, you cannot be sure of your own talents unless you are exposed to the opportunity to find your own special talent. Give your children the exposure to a variety of experiences in order to help them find their own special talent.

Appendix F

The Family Tree DNA ad on the next page is the company I used to process my DNA for testing. I highly recommend this site for 2 main reasons. The database used to match you with other individuals is extremely large and that will result in a higher possibility of finding matches. Secondly, the data they supply is more detailed and easier to understand than the results I have looked at for some of the other companies.

If you are interested in looking at the website on Family Tree DNA for the Nicely (Knisely, Knisley, Niceley, and other various spellings) you can go to the following link by typing it into the address line of your internet browser. There is a lot of information in the site and you can choose the differ sections and explore all the information that is posted there. I am the Administrator of the site and you can contact me if you have any questions. You can also search the site for other surnames if your male line you are looking for is not a Knusli line. On the main website page there is a block to search for surnames.

Nicely website link

https://www.familytreedna.com/public/Nicely/

Main Website Page for Family Tree DNA

https://www.familytreedna.com/

Once you are on this page select projects and you can then run a project search in the upper right hand corner of the page.

If you have any questions, the phone number and website help desk is located in the ad or you can contact Ron Nicely at nicelyguy@msn.com

The 50,000 Year DNA Journey of the Knusli Family

FamilyTree DNA
A Division of Gene by Gene

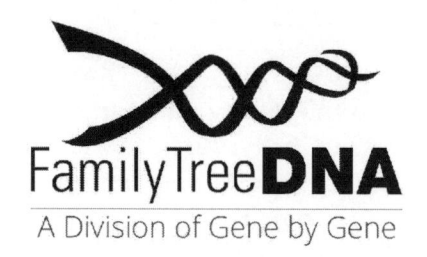

Where **TECHNOLOGY** and **HISTORY**
combine to uncover the story of you.

Use **Family Finder** to **discover your ethnic make-up** using the new myOrigins tool, **connect with close relatives** from both sides of your family tree, and **compare you and your matches' chromosomes directly.**

Y-DNA testing will **match** you to men that share a common ancestor on your father's line, **reveal the migratory path of your father's ancestors**, and includes **free participation in family and geographical research projects** run by our immense pool of Citizen Scientists. This test covers the Y chromosome and is available to men only.

mtDNA testing will **match** you to people that share a common ancestor on your mother's line, **reveal the migratory path of your mother's ancestors**, and also includes **free participation in family and geographical research projects** run by our dedicated Citizen Scientists.

World Headquarters
1445 North Loop West, Suite 820 Houston, Texas 77008, USA
Phone: (713) 868-1438
General and Media Inquiries:
helpdesk@familytreedna.com / media@familytreedna.com

Appendix G

In doing research on the family name in the Zurich Switzerland area, I found the following individuals and families. I cannot find a connection to Hans Knussli but I suspect these people are either ancestors or relatives of our Hans. If anyone ever locates any information on any of these individuals, please let me know.

1. Jagli or Jacob KNUESLI (KNUSLI) was born circa 1557 in Uster, Canton of Zurich, Switzerland. He died before 1637 at the age of 80.

Jagli or Jacob KNUESLI (KNUSLI) and Elsi BUENZLI were married on 1 Apr 1582 in Uster, Canton of Zurich, Switzerland. Elsi BUENZLI was born circa 1566. She died before 1646 at the age of 80.

Jagli or Jacob KNUESLI (KNUSLI) and Elsi BUENZLI had the following children:

- 2 i. Hans KNUESLI (KNUSLI) was born circa 1583. He was christened on 23 Jun 1583 in Uster, Canton of Zurich, Switzerland. He died before 1663 at the age of 80.
- 3 ii. Andreas KNUESLI (KNUSLI) was born circa 1584. He was christened on 19 Jan 1585 in Uster, Canton of Zurich, Switzerland. He died before 1664 at the age of 80.
- +4 iii. Marx KNUESLI (KNUSLI), born ca 1586; married Margretha ERISMANN, ca 1613, Uster, Canton of Zurich, Switzerland; died bef 1666.

1. Jagli KNUESLI (KNUSLI) was born circa 1617. He died before 1697 at the age of 80.

Jagli KNUESLI (KNUSLI) and Margreth BUENZLI were married on 16 Jan 1638 in Uster, Canton of Zurich, Switzerland. Margreth BUENZLI was born circa 1618. She died on 23 Feb 1676 at the age of 58 in Oberuster, Canton of Zurich, Switzerland.

Jagli KNUESLI (KNUSLI) and Margreth BUENZLI had the following children:

    2   i.   Dorothea KNUESLI (KNUSLI) was born circa 1638. She was christened on 4 Sep 1638 in Uster, Canton of Zurich, Switzerland. She died before 1718 at the age of 80.

    3   ii.   Hans Heinrich KNUESLI (KNUSLI) was born circa 1639. He was christened on 20 Oct 1639 in Uster, Canton of Zurich, Switzerland. He died before 1719 at the age of 80.

    4   iii.   Hans Caspar KNUESLI (KNUSLI) was born circa 1643. He was christened on 11 May 1643 in Uster, Canton of Zurich, Switzerland. He died circa 1644 at the age of 1.

    5   iv.   Hans Caspar KNUESLI (KNUSLI) was born circa 1645. He was christened on 29 Jun 1645 in Uster, Canton of Zurich, Switzerland. He died before 1725 at the age of 80.

    6   v.   Anna KNUESLI (KNUSLI) was born circa 1649. She was christened on 14 Jan 1649 in Uster, Canton of Zurich, Switzerland. She died before 1729 at the age of 80.

1. Hans KNUESLI (KNUSLI) was born circa 1619 in Maedikon, Canton of Zurich, Switzerland. He was christened on 2 May 1619 in Stallikon, Canton of Zurich, Switzerland. He died before 1699 at the age of 80.

Hans KNUESLI (KNUSLI) and Anna NAEF were married circa 1650 in Stallikon, Canton of Zurich, Switzerland. Anna NAEF, daughter of Hans NAEF and Barbara WISMER, was born circa 1628 in Stallikon, Canton of Zurich, Switzerland. She was christened on 2 Jun 1628 in Stallikon, Canton of Zurich, Switzerland. She died before 1710 at the age of 82.

Hans KNUESLI (KNUSLI) and Anna NAEF had the following children:

    2   i.   Jacob KNUESLI (KNUSLI) was born circa 1651 in Maedikon, Canton of Zurich, Switzerland. He died before 1731 at the age of 80.

    3   ii.   Elsbeth KNUESLI (KNUSLI) was born circa 1654 in Maedikon, Canton of Zurich, Switzerland. She was christened on 19 Dec 1654 in Stallikon, Canton of Zurich, Switzerland. She died before 1734 at the age of 80.

1. Hans Jagli KNUESLI (KNUSLI) was born circa 1572 in Uster, Canton of Zurich, Switzerland. He died before 1634 at the age of 62 in Oberuster, Canton of Zurich, Switzerland.

Hans Jagli KNUESLI (KNUSLI) and Margreth SALLENBACH were married circa 1593 in Uster, Canton of Zurich, Switzerland. Margreth SALLENBACH was born circa 1573 in Uster, Canton of Zurich, Switzerland. She died before 1653 at the age of 80.

Hans Jagli KNUESLI (KNUSLI) and Margreth SALLENBACH had the following children:

    2   i.   Felix KNUESLI (KNUSLI) was born circa 1593. He was christened on 28 Jul 1594 in Uster, Canton of Zurich, Switzerland. He died before 1673 at the age of 80.

    3   ii.   Regula KNUESLI (KNUSLI) was born circa 1596. She was christened circa 1597 in Oberuster, Canton of Zurich, Switzerland. She died before 1676 at the age of 80.

    4   iii.   Hans KNUESLI (KNUSLI) was born circa 1598. He was christened on 11 Jan 1599 in Uster, Canton of Zurich, Switzerland. He died before 1678 at the age of 80.

    5   iv.   Elsy KNUESLI (KNUSLI) was born circa 1600. She was christened in Feb 1601 in Uster, Canton of Zurich, Switzerland. She died before 1680 at the age of 80.

6	v.	Jagli KNUESLI (KNUSLI) was born circa 1605. He was christened on 22 Feb 1606 in Uster, Canton of Zurich, Switzerland. He died before 1670 at the age of 65.

1. Marx KNUESLI (KNUSLI) was born circa 1586. He was christened on 3 Feb 1587 in Uster, Canton of Zurich, Switzerland. He died before 1666 at the age of 80.

Marx KNUESLI (KNUSLI) and Margretha ERISMANN were married circa 1613 in Uster, Canton of Zurich, Switzerland. Margretha ERISMANN was born circa 1592 in Uster, Canton of Zurich, Switzerland. She died before 1672 at the age of 80.

Marx KNUESLI (KNUSLI) and Margretha ERISMANN had the following children:

2	i.	Hans Rudolph KNUESLI (KNUSLI) was born circa 1615 in Uster, Canton of Zurich, Switzerland. He was christened on 11 Jun 1616 in Uster, Canton of Zurich, Switzerland. He died before 1695 at the age of 80.
3	ii.	Hans Jagli KNUESLI (KNUSLI) was born circa 1618. He was christened on 2 Mar 1619 in Uster, Canton of Zurich, Switzerland. He died before 1698 at the age of 80.
4	iii.	Felix KNUESLI (KNUSLI) was born circa 1625. He was christened on 29 May 1626 in Uster, Canton of Zurich, Switzerland. He died before 1705 at the age of 80.

1. Hans Jacob KNUESSLI (KNUSLI) was born circa 1619 in Uster, Canton of Zurich, Switzerland. He was christened on 2 Mar 1619 in Uster, Canton of Zurich, Switzerland. He died on 28 Aug 1684 at the age of 65.

Hans Jacob KNUESSLI (KNUSLI) and Barbara HINDERMEISTER were married on 4 Aug 1646 in Uster, Canton of Zurich, Switzerland. Barbara HINDERMEISTER, daughter of Hans HINDERMEISTER and Ursula LAENNER, was born circa 1624. She was christened on 2 Jul 1624 in Gossau, Canton of Zurich, Switzerland. She died on 26 Nov 1682 at the age of 58.

Hans Jacob KNUESSLI (KNUSLI) and Barbara HINDERMEISTER had the following child:

 2 i. Anna KNUESSLI (KNUSLI) was born circa 1659. She was christened on 25 May 1660 in Uster, Canton of Zurich, Switzerland. She died on 3 Aug 1668 at the age of 9.

1. Hans KNUESSLI (KNUSLI) died before 1611. He was born circa 1631 in Stallikon, Canton of Zurich, Switzerland.

Hans KNUESSLI (KNUSLI) and Anna NAF were married before 1656 in Stallikon, Canton of Zurich, Switzerland. Anna NAF died before 1616. She was born circa 1636 in Stallikon, Canton of Zurich, Switzerland.

Hans KNUESSLI (KNUSLI) and Anna NAF had the following children:

 2 i. Madalena KNUESSLI (KNUSLI) was born circa 1655. She was christened on 30 Jan 1656 in Stallikon, Canton of Zurich, Switzerland. She died before 1735 at the age of 80.
 3 ii. Verena KNUESSLI (KNUSLI) died before 1636. She was born circa 1656. She was christened on 18 Jan 1657 in Stallikon, Canton of Zurich, Switzerland.
 4 iii. Hans KNUESSLI (KNUSLI) died before 1637. He was born circa 1657. He was christened on 12 Sep 1658 in Stallikon, Canton of Zurich, Switzerland.
 5 iv. Heinrich KNUESSLI (KNUSLI) was born circa 1660. He was christened on 23 May 1661 in Stallikon, Canton of Zurich, Switzerland. He died before 1740 at the age of 80.

+6   v.   Jos KNUESSLI (KNUSLI), born ca 1665; married Barbli STAHLI, 18 Oct 1690, Stallikon, Canton of Zurich, Switzerland; died bef 1745.

7   vi.   Anna KNUESSLI (KNUSLI) was born circa 1670. She was christened on 1 Jan 1671 in Stallikon, Canton of Zurich, Switzerland. She died before 1750 at the age of 80.

1. Jos KNUSLI (KNUSLI) was born circa 1605. He died before 1685 at the age of 80.

Jos KNUSLI (KNUSLI) and Elisabetha MUNCH were married circa 1626. Elisabetha MUNCH was born circa 1606. She died before 1686 at the age of 80.

Jos KNUSLI (KNUSLI) and Elisabetha MUNCH had the following child:

2   i.   Adam KNUSLI (KNUSLI) was born in 1627 in Leimbach, Canton of Zurich, Switzerland. He died before 1707 at the age of 80.

1. Hans KNUSLI (KNUSLI) was born circa 1567. He died before 1647 at the age of 80.

Hans KNUSLI (KNUSLI) and Elsbeth BAUR were married on 28 Jan 1588 in Stallikon, Canton of Zurich, Switzerland. Elsbeth BAUR was born circa 1568. She died before 1648 at the age of 80.

1. Jacob KNUSSLI (KNUSLI) was born circa 1775 in Oberuster, Canton of Zurich, Switzerland. He died circa 1800 at the age of 25 in Uster, Canton of Zurich, Switzerland.

Jacob KNUSSLI (KNUSLI) and Barbara BUNZLI were married circa 1799. Barbara BUNZLI was born circa 1779 in Oberuster, Canton of Zurich, Switzerland. She died circa 1800 at the age of 21 in Uster, Canton of Zurich, Switzerland.

Jacob KNUSSLI (KNUSLI) and Barbara BUNZLI had the following child:

2   i.   Anna Margaretha KNUSSLI (KNUSLI) was born circa 1801 in Uster, Canton of Zurich, Switzerland. She was christened on 9 Apr 1801 in Uster, Canton of Zurich, Switzerland. She died on 6 Jan 1864 at the age of 63 in Russikon, Canton of Zurich, Switzerland.

1. Hans Ulrich KNUSSLI (KNUSLI) was born circa 1600. He died before 1638 at the age of 38.

Hans Ulrich KNUSSLI (KNUSLI) and Margreth UNKNOWN were married circa 1635 in Canton of Zurich, Switzerland. Margreth UNKNOWN was born in 1619 in Canton of Zurich, Switzerland. She died circa 1635 at the age of 16 in Canton of Zurich, Switzerland.

References

Charles H. Glatfelter. *The Pennsylvania Germans. A Brief Account of their Influence on Pennsylvania*. Pennsylvania History Studies No. 20, The Pennsylvania Historical Association. University Park. Pennsylvania, 1990

Family Tree DNA. Genetic Genealogy Tutorials; World's Largest Testing facility for Genetic DNA: website www.familytreedna.com

James Shreeve. *The Greatest Journey*. New York, NY: National Geographic Society Magazine, March 2006. Pgs. 61-73

Lancaster Mennonite Historical Society. 2215 Millstream Road, Lancaster, PA 17602-1499. Maps and Historical Mennonite Family histories and files.

Ligonier Valley Library, 120 West Main St., Ligonier, PA 15658. PA Room files and family histories.

Microsoft® Encarta® Online Encyclopedia 2004, *Hessen*, http://encarta.msn.com © 1997-2004 Microsoft Corporation.

National Geographic Society. National Geographic Genographic Project. Online https://www3.nationalgeographic.com/genographic/report.html). Accessed January 2008

Richard Hooker, World Civilizations, Washington State University, Online at http://www.wsu.edu.

Skippack Historical Society, Skippack, PA, Mennonite Persecution and Migration to America, http://www.skippack.org/mennonite_persecution.htm

Dr. Spencer Wells, *The Journey of Man*, Princeton University Press, Princeton, New Jersey, 2002

Steven M. Nolt. *A History Of The Amish*. Good Books, Intercourse, Pennsylvania, 1968.

Swiss Mennonite Cultural and Historical Assn. The Palatinate, http://www.swissmennonite.org/history/history.html from The European History of the Swiss Mennonites from Volhynia; Schrag, Martin H 1956

APPENDIX H

Bible Ancestor Information

Information from Sidney Sachs on our Y-DNA in Jericho on June 28, 2014.

Sidney Sachs is a researcher of Hebrew line Y-DNA and also is the producer of the Public TV show "Tracing Your Family Roots" which has a lot of shows on DNA research. His Y-DNA and mine matched very closely several years ago and I mentioned that in the book. When I sent him a copy of my book, he responded with the following information on our family history. After receiving the information, I did some searching for Bible Genealogy information and was able to construct a family tree that I listed below the information Sidney supplied.

Sidney wrote, you should tell Jake Knisely that your ancestors were definitely outside the wall of Jericho, (see page 13 and 14) they also marched with Joshua around the wall each day. Why can I make that statement? It is in the Y-DNA. About 900 years ago, there was a mutation on one marker of 3 steps from your value. Everyone with that mutation who knew of his Jewish background, have the family history as being in the Jewish Priesthood line. That line is the paternal (male) line from Aaron, who was Moses' brother, knowing that Y-DNA is passed down from father to son, as explained in Y-DNA information.

The Bible quote in your book stated that the priests were carrying their ram's horns with Joshua. Who were the priests? They were the son and grandsons of Aaron. Since it was only 40 years after Aaron became high priest, the chances are high that they were few in number. Since your DNA is the same as my paternal ancestor from 1000 years ago, you also should be in Aaron paternal line. However, that line did not include David. Kings did not come from the priest line.

The Jewish Priesthood was started with Aaron and is passed down from each father to all of his sons. Every J2 Jew (about 100 of us) that have the mutation on DYS 455 from your value of 11 to 8 and have most of your Y-DNA have a family history of being Kohenim, which is the Jewish Priesthood line. This means that the persons with the mutation would likely have been a Kohenim. Since you have this mutation, your paternal line must be the same. Other DNA haplogroups also claim to be Kohenim. The one with the most members at 52% are the J1s, several persons using different methods dated it only going back to the time of the Second Temple or even later. J2s are the second largest group that are Kohenim and are dated back at least 3200 years. However, they are split between J2a and J2b. I am unable to check the dates from both these haplogroups. R1s that are Kohenim, are around 4% of the group, and are dated back to a time before Aaron. That's the reason I think your paternal line goes back to Jacob through his third son and not the fourth.

I asked Sidney the following question. How do you know Aaron has the same Y-DNA or how do you know he is your ancestor. Answer: The Y-DNA is passed from father to son. The same is true if you are a Jewish priest (Kohanim). The Jewish procedure of passing Priesthood from father to son started with Aaron and continued for all of these years. The Kohanim have a special honor in a Jewish Service, the first blessing before the reading of the Torah. There are other things, that they can and cannot do that others may or may not do. Also, our Jewish naming custom of "son of" included being a Kohanim at the end. That is how we kept our knowledge of who are the descendants of Aaron.

Following is the entire Male line from Adam to down to our ancestor Aaron, brother of Moses. Which in this case is the Y-DNA (J2 Haplogroup) of the Knusli family line. This was taken from information from Sidney Sachs and on the following websites.

http://www.complete-bible-genealogy.com/
and
http://www.biblebell.org/search.html

Adam   Wife Eve
Seth – Sheth
Enos – Enosh
Kenan - Cainan
Mahalalel – Maleael
Jared – Jered
Enoch – Henoch
Methuselah – Mathusala
Lamech
Noah – Noe
Shem – Sem
Arphaxad
Cainan
Shelah - Salah – Sala
Eber – Heber
Peleg – Phalec
Reu – Ragau
Serug – Saruch
Nahor – Nachor   (Wife) Milkah
Terah – Thara (See Bible quote in my book on page 12)
Abram – Abraham   (Wife) Sarai – Sarah
Isaac   (Wife) Rebekah
Jacob – Israel   (Wife) Leah
Levi   (Wife) Milkah
Kohath
Amram   (Wife) Jochebed
Aaron (his brother was Moses and his sister was Miriam) (Wife) Elsheba